*Praise for Gary Joseph Grappo*

## THE TOP 10 CAREER STRATEGIES FOR THE YEAR 2000 & BEYOND

"The job market may be changing at the speed of light, but Gary Grappo offers the kind of insight and guidance that can help you keep up—and get ahead."

—Peter Brown, Chairman, Four Seasons Group, Inc.

"Gary Grappo has always been a source of good, sound career advice. Now he turns his attention to the changing job market and the prospects for tomorrow—and, as always, give his readers information they can really use."

—Paul Poissant, Director of M.B.A. Professional Development, The Smeal College of Business, Pennsylvania State University

"This book provides excellent ideas for those who are starting out, starting over, or starting to prepare for the future."

—Daniel L. Carricato, Vice President, Human Resources, Hilton Resorts Corporation

## GET THE JOB YOU WANT IN THIRTY DAYS

"Don't interview without this book! It's loaded with simple, straightforward advice that can make all the difference in getting the job."

—Gloria Rozen Koznesoff, John Hancock Financial Services

"From writing the resume to clinching the job, this book takes you step-by-step and tells you what to do to succeed."

—Leon N. Graham, Executive Vice President, BMG Direct

## THE TOP 10 FEARS OF JOB SEEKERS

"An excellent resource for turning career stress into career success."

—Scott DeGarmo, Editor-in-Chief and Publisher, *Success* magazine

"Gary Grappo goes beyond typical self-help clichés to offer truly valuable guidance for the job hunter."

—Robert K. Prescott, Director, Corporate Services and Instructor in Business Administration, The Smeal College of Business, Pennsylvania State University

*Berkley Books by Gary Joseph Grappo*

START YOUR OWN BUSINESS IN THIRTY DAYS

THE TOP 10 CAREER STRATEGIES FOR THE YEAR 2000 & BEYOND

GET THE JOB YOU WANT IN THIRTY DAYS

THE TOP 10 FEARS OF JOB SEEKERS

# START YOUR OWN BUSINESS IN THIRTY DAYS

## GARY JOSEPH GRAPPO

Berkley Books, New York

This book is an original publication of The Berkley Publishing Group.

START YOUR OWN BUSINESS IN THIRTY DAYS

A Berkley Book / published by arrangement with the author

PRINTING HISTORY
Berkley trade paperback edition / August 1998

The Penguin Putnam Inc. World Wide Web site address is
http://www.penguinputnam.com

ISBN: 0-425-16322-9

BERKLEY®
Berkley Books are published by The Berkley Publishing Group, a member of
Penguin Putnam Inc.,
200 Madison Avenue, New York, New York 10016.
BERKLEY and the "B" design
are trademarks belonging to Berkley Publishing Corporation.

PRINTED IN THE UNITED STATES OF AMERICA
10 9 8 7 6 5 4 3 2 1

*This book is dedicated to you, the reader.*
*To each one who brings this thirty-day plan to life and makes it happen.*

# CONTENTS

# CHARTS AND EXERCISES

# ACKNOWLEDGMENTS

The following are business owners I know, family and friends from whom I have learned much through the years. Many started and continue to operate businesses out of their homes. Others have grown well beyond their humble beginnings.

Jacques Aboaf, list broker

Peter and Susan Brown, resort lodge owners

Pema and Perry Browne, literary agents

Tasso Chriss, Italian shoe importer

BJ and Michael Davis, bed and breakfast inn owners

Shelley DeMaio, women's apparel fashion representative

Dan Discher, business phone and shipping cost reduction consultant

John Dunn, publisher and agent for dramatists

Ken Ellens, marketing consultant

Peter Friedrich, inn owner

Pat Galvin, freelance writer of company newsletters

Truxtun Gowen, career consultant

Jim and Paula Grappo, real estate developers/golf ball brokers

Bruce Marks, personal coach and trainer for ice hockey players

Helga Harris, canvas artist and designer of wearable art

Linda Heneson, neighborhood package and shipping store owner

John Jamieson, addiction and codependency therapist

Rick Langnas, sports agent for professional athletes

Matt Merkel, commercial graphic artist

Jack Paget, personal fitness trainer

Don Parsons, designer and builder of log homes

Tom Pye, private family practice attorney at law

Nancy Rehbine, human resource training consultant

Jorgen Roed, hotel conference center owner

Maryann Rogers, beauty shop owner

Louie Salaben, real estate agent

Joyce Spiegel, business gifts and employee awards specialist

Andre Torres, chef and small restaurant owner

And anyone else I may have forgotten...

# INTRODUCTION

In *Start Your Own Business in Thirty Days,* Gary Joseph Grappo has cut through the complex formulas of starting a business and created a practical, easy-to-follow guide. Most important, he has formulated a daily action plan for you. This plan, when properly executed, virtually guarantees you will start your own business in thirty days or less. The key to achieving your objective is to utilize Mr. Grappo's plan. If you follow this plan daily, you will realize your goal.

Gary Joseph Grappo is founder and former president of CareerEdge, leaders of career seminars for major colleges and universities and job fairs nationwide. In the past twenty-five years, he has launched over sixteen businesses and speaks in this book from a wealth of entrepreneurial experiences. Mr. Grappo is also author of *The Top 10 Career Strategies for the*

*Year 2000 and Beyond, Get the Job You Want in Thirty Days, The Top 10 Fears of Job Seekers,* contributing writer to *The Wall Street Journal's National Business Employment Weekly, The Chicago Tribune* and the *Fort Lauderdale Sun-Sentinel* and coauthor of the career best-seller *How to Write Better Resumes.*

*Start Your Own Business in Thirty Days* is the result of years of expertise brought to you in an easy-to-follow system. Along with learning how to utilize your Daily Activity Planner, you will discover:

**1.** Why having defined goals is important and how to assess your skills and interests to discover the business that is right for you

**2.** The importance of a positive attitude and how to maintain that attitude even when the going gets tough

**3.** How to create a simple but successful business plan for your new venture

**4.** Effective ways to play the "numbers game" to generate sales through creative face-to-face networking as well as how to utilize the Internet's on-line resources to market your company

**5.** What you should and should not do on a client sales call

**6.** The importance of follow-up and how to use it effectively

# FOREWORD

About the home...

There are more than 200 million people in the United States and over 40 million homes for them to buy. "It used to be that home was a place to stay in, and enjoy," states Andy Rooney. It still is, but in the later part of the twentieth century a new dimension in home living has evolved: home-based businesses. With the growth in technology such as the desktop computer, fax machines, on-line services and the Internet, the home has begun to evolve more and more as a place of business too. After all, what else are we going to do with all that extra space in our homes? Rooney jokingly reminisces in his book, *The Most of Andy Rooney:*

> The house had been built by a carpenter who did it from a plan in his head. There are rooms in our houses

that weren't designed for anything special. Usually homes were built with four or five bedrooms, a living room, a parlor, a big kitchen, but then there were spare rooms. The builder didn't have any idea what you were going to do with your spare room. It wasn't his business. You could make up what the room was for as you went along living. Then there was always one floor above the top floor, too, the attic. An attic was maybe the best place ever invented for a house and it's too bad they're a thing of the past.

By now, some of these same or similar thoughts may have crossed your mind a time or two. You, like Rooney, have probably asked the question. How can I best utilize the rooms or space that I have in my home; more important, how can I utilize them to start my own business?

I once started a half-million-dollar business on a typewriter in the corner of my bedroom. Writing this book comes from the experience of starting sixteen businesses in the past twenty-five years. I'm currently starting my seventeenth.

This is a practical and realistic guide to starting your own business in thirty days. It is the result of personal trial and error and a sincere desire to help others. I'm not a genius. If I can do it, you can do it too! Take this system and make it your success. Success! Yes, success!

# HOW TO USE THIS BOOK

B ecause this is a thirty-day process, it is important that the book is read in sequential order. The chapters are laid out in such a fashion that a building process evolves. What you get from this book depends on the same principles utilized by home builders and bricklayers: brick by brick, the foundation must be solid. The full significance of the thirty key concepts will be realized when each step is understood, accepted and acted upon before moving on to the next.

When you have read the book in its entirety, your work has only just begun. Immediately make daily use of the Activity Planner. Ideas are simply that—ideas—until they are acted upon. The Activity Planner, besides giving you an action plan, also contains a quick reference of the thirty key concepts that are fundamental to your success. The quick reference is provided to help you reduce pages of information to key essentials that should be acted upon.

When you read this book in sequential order and implement the Activity Planner, you are on the road to success. You have all the tools you need to start your own business and make your own declaration of independence.

# START YOUR
## OWN BUSINESS
### IN THIRTY DAYS

---
 1 
---

# TAKE PERSONAL INVENTORY AND DISCOVER THE BUSINESS THAT'S RIGHT FOR YOU

N ot long after I wrote *Get The Job You Want in Thirty Days*, an enormous realization came to me: not all individuals, myself included, want to work for an employer. Whether you're just starting out or in transition as the result of corporate uprighting (politically correct for "corporate downsizing"), many of you would prefer to own your own business and work from home. Statistically, this is an accurate assumption. Most research points to the fact that up to 75 percent of employed personnel have thought about owning or have a strong desire to own their own business.

In just ten years of my career, I worked for a wide variety of companies, ranging from airlines to hotels and computer manufacturers. Some of them went bankrupt, others downsized. As a result of job insecurity, I became good at getting a job. I don't regret the time spent working for any one of my former employers. Each employer provided valuable work and life experience. But, for the most part, something inside of me rejects the thought of ever working for another employer, dealing with their ups and downs and in many cases becoming just another insignificant casualty on the road to their success. I like my independence. Theoretically, I have no bosses except for clients, and I make all my own decisions. The freedom of being in control of both my life and career is exhilarating. I prefer being self-employed. In fact, according to research, independence and being in control are the number one reasons why entrepreneurs prefer self-employment. Money is number two.

As for so many others, the happiest times in my life have been when I've been on my own, working from home. The challenge, of course, has always been how to come up with a strong business idea in order to produce enough income so as to pay the bills and ward off the I-better-get-a-job insecurity blues. And the business idea has to be implemented with little or no money, but yet be strong enough to generate substantial income within thirty, maximum sixty, days. Now, that is a real challenge!

Starting your own business and generating immediate income is not as difficult as it may sound if you begin your quest with some serious introspection. With a good self-assessment and a clear understanding of what you like to do, and by following the plan set forth in this book, almost any of you can start your own profitable business.

## TAKE PERSONAL INVENTORY: WHAT DO YOU LIKE TO DO?

The first priority in this process is to start a business that is firmly based on something you like to do. If you have a love and passion for something, that passion becomes the fuel to make your business succeed. A pastor friend, well-known author and speaker from Princeton Theological Seminary Leonard Evans, once provoked a reaction from me in guiding my career with the question "If you had your druthers—forget about money, opportunity or the right connections—what would you be doing with your life right now?" Good question. What would you be doing with your life right now? What makes you the happiest?

### Hobbies

A few years ago, on a Friday night, friends gathered at my home to enjoy what was another one of my now famous, better-than-any-restaurant meals (so they say). Let me preface the story by saying that for about a year, in my spare time, I had been going to the main library in downtown Miami and checking out instructional cooking videos. Thanks to Julia Child and others, I learned how to cook extremely well, and used my friends to experiment on as I was being self-taught. Don't feel sorry for them, they didn't mind it.

On this particular Friday night, while dining on Coq au Vin for main course and a death-by-chocolate almond torte for dessert, the group suggested, jokingly, that I be invited to cook like this at their homes any night of the week they needed me. After all, they surmised, the food was excellent, better than any restaurant, and we all got to dine in the comfort of a home environment.

By Saturday evening I had drafted a business plan to promote an in-home chef service called *YPC—Your Personal Chef.* The company I had been working for had just folded days earlier and I was out of a job. I needed a quick, viable solution to generate money and pay the bills. In my heart and my gut, I knew *YPC* was it.

On Monday morning only three days later, bright and early, I was out cold calling; meeting with the doormen of the most elegant buildings in Miami. To each I gave a stack of flyers I had designed on my home computer, legitimizing *YPC* as a business. Next, I offered each doorman a sales commission for every referral in his building that became a client. I had my first *YPC* private-duty chef job within three days. Within the first thirty days I had grossed $3,000!

To make hobbies work for you, as I did with *YPC,* assess your personal hobbies and interests. Take note of them mentally. Write them down in a list. Don't forget to consider every one, from the most obvious passion to the most remote interest. Each has potential for becoming a business. Next, after you complete your list, explore, brainstorm, and think about how you can make your hobbies and interests become the basis of your very own profitable business.

If you can't think of any hobbies or interests, begin now to foster some new ones. It's unfortunate that many of us live our lives passively glued to our TV sets, and still others excessively affixed to computers, in on-line chat rooms. When was the last time you tried something new? When was the last time you took the initiative to go to the library or buy a book to learn something new? As can be seen in the case of *YPC,* if you take the time to cultivate a new interest, it can become the basis for a business driven by the fuel of personal passion. At some point in the future it can become a cash-producing opportunity just when you need it.

## Training

In one of my many careers, in the employ of various companies, I've been more than once a corporate director of human resource training and development. It was no secret to me that most employees detested the most dreaded exercise of all—attending training seminars. As director of training, I myself had to admit that in most cases I did not enjoy sitting in a classroom getting information crammed into my head either.

But training is like medicine—sometimes you've just got to swallow it and take it because it's good for you. Through the sometimes painful process of learning something new, we open ourselves to endless possibilities. Most important, the more information we acquire, the greater the chances are of our taking that information and someday using it to start a business. After all, why not tap into free and new information given to us by our employers and make good use of it for ourselves as well?

One such incident happened to me when, early in my career, I signed on as a sales representative in the computer division of Lanier Business Systems. The new "sales cadets" nationwide were shipped off to Atlanta for two weeks of "basic training." Anyone that has worked for Lanier knows what I am talking about. Picture an enclosed compound with housing, food service and, yes, lots of trainers and training rooms. While learning computers and sales skills for two weeks straight, the rules included: no alcohol at any time on campus, up at 6 A.M., training classes all day, after-dinner group role-plays and team work until 10 P.M., a passing grade on all tests and no spouses or friends on campus until training was over.

By the end of the two weeks, the general mood was "I hate training." I include myself in that. It was hard to see anything good out of what we had just been through.

A couple years later, however, Lanier computers had rocky times and eventually the company closed its Miami office. I had been in food service all through high school and college and fell back on it working as a waiter at the Biltmore Restaurant in Coral Gables to keep money coming in while I was unemployed.

Being a food server was different this time; especially after all the sales training I had just been through at Lanier. I began to use my sales skills to upsell desserts, wines, and as they say in the sales business, add-ons. My tips were phenomenal.

Long story short, I started a company from all the Lanier sales training I had just been through. It was called TipsPlus. I went from restaurant to hotel to more restaurants all around South Florida selling a food-server training program I had written on my home computer to help food servers increase their check and tip amounts. It was a win-win product. It helped the establishment be more profitable and it increased the servers' tips. It worked. Eventually it grew into an expanded training products company selling hundreds of thousands of dollars in service training programs over the past ten years. More on that later.

In summary, don't be afraid of attending training programs. Enroll in them. Pay for them yourself. Just go and do it. Take stock in the training you have received to date. Make a list. How can you take what you have learned and create a moneymaking business opportunity for youself now?

## Experience

As I mentioned in the foreword, as I write this book I am starting my seventeenth business. In fact, I'll share more about this unique venture in chapter 3. Brian Tracy, author of the audiotape series *The Science of Self-Confidence*, has researched that on an average, self-made entrepreneurial millionaires have started sixteen businesses. It's good to know I'm normal. As a result of starting seventeen businesses, I've had lots of experiences and you'll have to excuse the many stories I have to share from time to time. But hopefully they will inspire you. In sharing them, I hope you will learn from the stories and receive time- and money-saving ideas as you embark on starting your own business.

In trying to discover the business that is right for you, besides exploring your hobbies and training, consider your life experiences. Somewhere hidden in all of your experiences may be the keys to the business that will make you happy and make you money.

As a child, I often heard my father speak of families in France whom he had met during the war. He received letters from them, especially at holiday times. He struggled with reading their letters scribbled in a foreign language none of us understood. As a result, I was determined to speak French someday.

After college, I began to make repeated trips to France to meet his friends from the war. I still had never studied French, but I began to learn it simply by living with the families in their homes. Within a few visits I was conversational. Within a couple years more, and after attending the Alliance Française in Miami, Florida, I began to also write in French and understand grammar.

My newfound French culture experiences began to lead me to the French islands of the Caribbean, and one in particular I enjoyed the most, St. Martin. Out of these experiences evolved not only a love for a new culture and language, but a business opportunity as well. The Hotel Alizea that I frequented on the island was so new, charming and delightful that I decided to start a business promoting tourism from the New York area to this wonderful French getaway. It all happened because I was able to communicate with the owners, who spoke only French, and thus learned of their need for a stateside sales representative. What an extremely rewarding and fun business opportunity that was, all born out of life experience.

Assess your life experiences. Go back as far as you can. What did you love as a child? Where did you go that was memorable? What experiences have accumulated over time to make you the person you are today? There are some hidden keys there that will unlock your next profitable business idea.

In *Get the Job You Want in Thirty Days*, I shared a story about someone very famous who took her passion, hobby and life experience and became wealthy almost instantly upon acting on her desires. I must share her story again here, now.

It's the story of a great pioneer woman. You may remember her legend. As a child, she asked her parents for a set of paints and brushes. Her interest in painting was dismissed as costly and foolish. Instead, as a young teenager she was married off to an older gentleman and she raised a large family. When she was a seventy-five-year-old widow, she decided to do what she had always loved; she decided to paint. Within five years, she established American primitive art as a style. She became known as Grandma Moses. After an exhibit at the Metropolitan Museum of Art and other exhibits around the nation, some of her work began to sell for over $100,000 a painting. The sale of one painting yielded her more money in a day than she and her husband had made in a lifetime.

## DO YOU HAVE WHAT IT TAKES TO OWN YOUR OWN BUSINESS?

Before starting your own business, you probably have hesitations about it as a result of repeatedly asking yourself the question "Am I the type?" Through the following test, you will be able to self-assess whether you have the personal traits to be a business owner. After all, you are the most important employee you will ever hire. You need to be reasonably sure that you will make a good hire. Answer the following questions truthfully. There are instructions on how to score yourself at the end of the test.

## TAKE THE ENTREPRENEUR TEST

Respond to each of the following questions. Circle the alphabet letter A, B, or C that best describes your behavior, feeling, or attitude as it actually is, not the way you wish it to be in response to the question. In order to get valid results, you must be absolutely honest!

---

**1.** *Are you enthusiastic and excited about new projects?*
   A. I love anything new. I am very adventurous.

B. If someone jumps in with me, I enjoy it.

C. Don't rush me. I'll get to it when I can.

2. *Do you like being around other people?*

A. I have lots of friends and can get along with anybody.

B. I like people, but sometimes I wish they'd leave me alone.

C. Most people you can't trust. You have to rely on yourself.

3. *How do you feel about leading and managing a group of people?*

A. I can get results out of people, and they even still like me.

B. I can get results out of people, but run into difficulties.

C. I usually let someone else do the moving and the shaking.

4. *How do you handle responsibility?*

A. There isn't anything I can't handle. I'm ready for anything.

B. I'll work hard, but I have my limits.

C. If there's someone else who will do it, let them.

5. *How good are you at time management and organization?*

A. I work from a "to do list" and like to have a plan.

B. I know what I'm supposed to do by instinct and I do it.

C. I take life and work as it comes. It's the only way to live.

6. *How do you view your work?*
    A. I love it. I don't mind working long and hard hours.
    B. I'll work, but don't push me.
    C. Hard work really doesn't get you anywhere.

7. *What is your decision-making style?*
    A. I can make up my mind quickly. No regrets here.
    B. I need time to make decisions, but I will eventually get to it.
    C. I don't like it. I usually mess things up.

8. *Can people trust you?*
    A. I always deliver exactly what I say. People count on me.
    B. I try, but sometimes I say what they want to hear.
    C. Who cares? Things change, people will have to deal with it.

9. *Can you make a long-term commitment?*
    A. Once I start something, I stick with it until completion.
    B. Once I start something, I get restless, but eventually finish.
    C. Why spin your wheels? Bail out if it's not working.

**10.** *What's your record on keeping records?*

   A. Both are important, get the work done and keep records.

   B. I'll do it, but I really don't like it.

   C. They're not important. I know exactly what's going on.

You're done…

## Scoring

Add up your total by using this scoring:
A=10 B=5 C=1

## Answer Key

**Score 100**

**Excellent.** A perfect score! You've got what it takes. Go for it! Start your own business; days, nights, weekends—do whatever it takes. You are virtually guaranteed financial and personal independence.

**Score 75–99**

**Very good.** You can do it. You may feel challenged at times, but you have the ability to overcome adversity and be a winner in the end. Owning your own business is definitely a viable option for you.

### Score 50–74

**Good.** You've got some of the qualities to be a small business owner, but some weak points to overcome too. You can identify your weak areas by rereading the test and comparing your answers to the letter A response for each question. The letter A represents the most effective skills and behaviors needed to be an entrepreneur. You can overcome your deficiencies by having a friend or spouse help you out in your weak areas. You could also consider professional training to prepare you.

### Score 25–49

**Below average**. You probably would not make it owning your own business. Find out why by comparing your answers to the letter A response for each question. The letter A represents the most effective skills and behaviors needed to be an entrepreneur. If you work hard and prepare to overcome these deficiencies through training, you may be ready at a later date.

### Score 24 and below

**Unsatisfactory.** Owning your own business is not for you. Why throw your life into turmoil when a job with a steady paycheck is what you need to keep you safe and secure. You don't need all the risks and problems that go with owning your own business.

## THE SKILLS YOU MOST ENJOY INVENTORY

Now that, hopefully, you have discovered you have what it takes to be self-employed, let's take an inventory of the skills you most enjoy using. In the following exercise, write on the left side the skills or jobs you most enjoy. On the right side list the jobs or experiences you do not enjoy. Consider your past work history, hobbies, volunteer and life experiences. Be as *detailed* and *specific* as you can.

| Enjoy | Do Not Enjoy |
|---|---|
| Examples:   Sales | Working outdoors |
| Teaching | Data-base management |
| Computers | Copy-editing |

## YOUR TOP 10 BUSINESS IDEA LIST

The inventory you just completed, combined with the analysis of your hobbies, training and life experiences that was laid out in the first few pages of this chapter, will help you create a list of viable business opportunities, one of which you will launch with this book's thirty-day action plan.

In the following exercise, make a list of ten business ideas that are congruent with your self-analysis. To help you brainstorm, consider seeking opinions from other sources. Possibly invite a few key friends over for a wine and cheese party, or for some beer and pizza—whatever works for you. Have fun with the group. Listen to their ideas and suggestions. Also, go to the bookstore or library and review lists of home-based business ideas in books that other entrepreneurs have published. Now you're ready to fill in the following blanks.

## MY PERSONAL TOP 10 BUSINESS IDEAS

1.

2.

3.

4.

5.

6.

7.

8.

9.

10.

After you have completed the above list, review your business ideas. Prioritize the list. To the right of each idea rank it in numerical order, the number 1 being the most viable opportunity and the number 10 being the least favorable. You now are very close to finalizing the home-based business that is right for you. In the rest of this book, we will follow a thirty-day plan to implement it. Welcome to the world of being a small business owner.

---
| **2** |
---

# START WITH A
# POSITIVE ATTITUDE

There's always someone who is going to tell you it can't be done; that you won't be able to implement the business idea you have decided upon. Of course, that someone should definitely not be you. History is filled with tales of people who were convinced their ideas would succeed. But it is also filled with people telling them they would not succeed.

Even the great Thomas Edison advised his friend Henry Ford to forget trying to make a motorcar. Edison was so convinced that the automobile idea was an impossibility, he invited Ford to come work for him. Ford believed in himself and in his idea. He was resolute and would not give up. The result of his powerfully positive attitude? Success.

"Leave flying to the birds," said the father and friends of Orville and Wilbur Wright. "What a silly and insane way to spend money," said the journalists and armed forces specialists who were locked into the thinking of their day. As a result, the Wright brothers set out to disprove those who laughed at their dream of building a flying machine. They launched their "foolish" idea at Kitty Hawk, North Carolina, and in the great scope of history, not many years later their belief landed a man on the moon!

The mind is the beginning of the reality you create for yourself. The result of positive thinking is a *positive reality*. The result of negative thinking is a *negative reality*. The single most important thing you can do for yourself in starting your own business is to absolutely believe that you can do it and that you will succeed.

**1** | **If you think you can or can't, in either case you're probably right.**

As you embark on your new business idea, catch yourself when you are self-absorbed, possibly when driving your car or lying awake at night and talking to yourself. These thoughts, this internal chatter is called *self-talk*. When we speak negatively to ourselves, what might it sound like? "I can't. It won't work. Maybe I should give up. I'm worried. I'm scared." You know the rhetoric. We all do it. The list could go on and on.

# 2 Practice positive self-talk: "I can! I will! I know I can do it!"

Many people that attend my seminars agree in principle that a positive attitude is a winning attitude. But most people do not know how to escape the destructive forces of negative self-talk. How do you do it? How can you maintain a positive and successful attitude when your friends, your family and even your own head are telling you that your business idea is "foolish" or that "it won't work"? The answer is simple, but revolutionary in its power; it is this: replace your negative internal chatter with positive winning statements. Try it. It sounds easy, but it truly is difficult to do, that is until you get used to a whole new way of talking to yourself. Once you form the new habit of learning to speak positively to yourself, it will take less and less conscious effort. But initially, be prepared, being positive does take conscious work. It's like training a muscle that you haven't used in a while, it will strain and hurt, but you will see it grow in time.

The following is a sample list of fifty positive-muscle-building affirmations that you can use to replace your negative self-talk. Use them as you daydream or lie awake thinking in your bed, or as you prepare to get up and start your day. Use them to replace any negative internal chatter you catch yourself using. Use them to reprogram your mind for success.

## 50 POSITIVE MUSCLE BUILDING
## AFFIRMATIONS

*I'm getting better at remembering people's names.*

*It's going to be a great day.*

*I know I can do it.*

*I know it's going to work.*

*Everything works together for the good.*

*I'm lucky, most of the time things fall my way.*

*I'm willing to try anything.*

*I have the talent to succeed.*

*I can learn how to do it.*

*I'm very creative.*

*Everything I eat is going to be the right nutritious choices today.*

*I'm never going to give up!*

*I'll keep trying until I make it work.*

*It won't take long to get organized.*

*Today is going to be my day, I can just feel it.*

*The money is going to be there when I need it.*

*I like it.*

*As long as I try, I can do anything.*

*I can lose the weight I want.*

*I'll have plenty of time to get it all done.*

*I have the patience to do it right.*

*This is really making my day.*

*I love Mondays.*

*I learn from all my mistakes.*

*Facing anything that comes my way is the challenge I love.*
*Just thinking about it gets me excited.*
*Sometimes I think, Damn I'm good.*
*I'm the best!*
*I love people.*
*I like the respect I get from others.*
*Getting up to speak in front of others is exciting.*
*I love cold calling.*
*I'm not afraid to take a chance.*
*I can quit smoking.*
*Things are working out for me right now.*
*I have all the energy I need to succeed.*
*I'm really getting into the best physical shape ever.*
*I am getting better and better at managing my money.*
*I love standing up in front of people and making presentations.*
*I'm good at anything I put my mind to.*
*I'll promote my business and meet my sales goals with no problems.*
*My desk is always organized.*
*I always can find things.*
*The best kind of luck is when I plan and work hard too.*
*I always win when I put my mind to it.*
*I never lose.*
*I'm never over the hill, I'm just getting better.*
*I usually beat the competition.*
*I have lots of friends.*
*I'll start a prosperous and profitable business,* I have no doubt.

By utilizing this life-changing principle of replacing negative self-talk with the positive self-talk described above, you can be assured you'll be among the winners in life. You can break old habits.

**3** Neutralize negative self-talk ("I'm worried. This business will never work.") with positive winning statements.

You can learn more about self-talk and the impact it has on your life by visiting the World Wide Web site of Dr. Shad Helmstetter, an authority on the topic of self-talk. Go to http://www.monsoon.org. Once you have arrived, scroll down to *The Self-talk Solution*. Click on its icon and you're on your way to learning how to create more positive internal chatter, resulting in a positive reality for your life and business.

**4** Don't wait for others. Take personal responsibility for creating and implementing your own business.

I'd like to share a poem that has meant a lot to me as I have started various businesses over the years. It has helped me to take personal responsibility for my own success and avoid listening to family and friends who have tried to rob me of my dreams. I have had to fight not only my own negative feelings, but also the negative comments of the people around me.

## IT COULDN'T BE DONE

Somebody said that it couldn't be done,
But he with a chuckle replied
That "maybe it couldn't," but he would be one
Who wouldn't say so till he'd tried.
So he buckled right in with the trace of a grin
On his face. If he worried he hid it.
He started to sing as he tackled the thing
That couldn't be done, and he did it.

Somebody scoffed: "Oh, you'll never do that;
At least no one ever has done it";
But he took off his coat and took off his hat,
And the first thing we knew he'd begun it.
With a lift of his chin and a bit of a grin,
Without any doubting or quittit,
He started to sing as he tackled the thing
That couldn't be done, and he did it.

There are thousands to tell you it cannot be done,
There are thousands to prophesy failure;
There are thousands to point out to you one by one,
The dangers that wait to assail you.
But just buckle in with a bit of a grin,
Then take off your coat and go to it;
Just start in to sing as you tackle the thing
That "cannot be done," and you'll do it.

—Edgar A. Guest

"Adversity is a fact of life," states Kitty, a clinical psychologist and graduate of Penn State University. "I've been in clinical psychology for twenty years now and I'm currently making the transition into business-to-business consulting. I'm starting my own executive coaching consulting company. It's not easy." For Kitty, shedding the stigma of being thought of as a clinical psychologist by those in the local business and social circles has been extremely difficult. "I take two steps forward and a step backward. It's times like this, when I fall off the horse, that I realize I need to get back on and ride harder. I keep telling myself that adversity in any start-up business venture is not unusual."

The Brooklyn Bridge spanning the East River tying Manhattan to Brooklyn, was just an idea in the mind of engineer John Roebling in 1883. What is little known of this spectacular undertaking is that many bridge builders throughout the world told him it would be impossible to build.

Roebling and his son Washington, a young engineer, together set out to achieve their dream despite criticism. Only a few months into the project, a serious accident at the site took the life of John Roebling and left Washington severely injured, with serious brain damage. With Washington unable to walk or talk, the general consensus of the workers was to give up on the project since their leaders were no longer there to support them.

Unable to move or talk, Washington still had a mind that was clear as a bell. Lying in his hospital bed, he had an idea. He could develop a code communication system as he moved one finger touching the arm of his wife. Tapping out the code, he could tell the engineers how to finish building the bridge. Thirteen years later, and after a lot of code tapping, despite adversity of the highest magnitude, one's man dream, his idea, was finally realized.

Winners understand that adverse circumstances are a fact of life. Voltaire, the great French philosopher, likened life to being dealt a hand of cards. What you personally do with the cards determines your success.

5 | **Practice visualization. When you lie awake in the morning or evening, visualize working at and enjoying your own business.**

Visualization is essentially a rehearsal for your own personal play called *Success*. An actor would never dream of going on stage without rehearsing his or her part. In order to be successful in your drama, you need to first of all rehearse in your mind and visualize your success. Shakti Gawain, in her book *Creative Visualization*, coaches you on how to effectively visualize. If there is one book you ever invest in, this is the one I suggest.

The business that I am starting as I write this book is called the American Hockey Association, and visualization has played a key role in its success. While I fall asleep at night, I visualize different aspects of the company. For instance, one night I visualized what our corporate head-quarters will look like here in Fort Lauderdale, Florida. I formed a mental image of a corporate head office with an ice and roller rink in it for the purpose of holding national train-ing clinics, as well as for employees to play hockey before and after work and on weekends. Through visualization, I've already seen what our logo and some of our products and services for members will look like. As I lie awake at night, I picture in my mind being president of the fastest-growing sport association in America.

With visualization, you can take positive action to assure a positive attitude. See yourself working successfully at the ideal business that you want to develop. Replay various sce-narios of how different aspects of the business will demon-strate success. Now write down ten mental pictures of suc-cess, similarly to what I just shared above. What are you going to visualize?

## CREATIVE VISUALIZATION:
## TEN MENTAL PICTURES OF SUCCESS

1.

2.

3.

4.

5.

6.

7.

8.

9.

10.

Every day you should visualize the ten pictures you just described. Add to them often, and get quality quiet time to visualize them.

**6**

> **Sell image! Dress like a winner.**
> **Shine your shoes. Have a conservative**
> **hairstyle. Design quality printed**
> **materials.**

As Will Rogers said, "You never get a second chance to make a first impression." Your business image must be clean, professional and essentially flawless in order to sell you and your company effectively.

According to research, verbal content comprises only 7 percent of your total message. Your visual image comprises 93 percent of the message you convey to others. What you say is only a small percent of what others perceive you to be.

Your personal image is projected in many and various ways as you encounter prospective clients and customers. Whether you realize it or not, customers are making judgements about you, either good or bad, by observing your image. Their impression of you, within the first thirty seconds of meeting you, will determine whether they will buy your product or service. Consider the following first impressions list before representing your business.

## FIRST IMPRESSIONS LIST

- A professional wardrobe; avoid flashy styles and colors
- Well-trimmed hair and neat styling

- Polished shoes
- A firm handshake
- A friendly smile
- Good posture
- Confidence and enthusiasm
- Good voice projection and diction
- Correct grammar and language usage
- Inviting tone of voice and pitch
- Excellent-quality printed materials
- A neat, clean and professional office

Why is making a good first impression according to this list so important? A negative first impression makes it difficult, if not impossible, to sell, influence or persuade someone. While starting or even maintaining your own business, you cannot afford not to have the right image to influence others, network and generate sales. Your image is first and foremost the main ingredient of your success.

When I launched the food server training consulting business TipsPlus and later the customer service program for service-related industries called Guest*Star, I went door to door selling it, literally. Since I had no background in organizational development or human resource training and development at that point in my career, by all sense of reason, the business should have never got off the ground. But one thing I did right, I dressed the part. Each day, I got in my car with the right image and drove to restaurants and hotels, from Orlando to Key West, Florida. I dressed as though I were employed by one of the top firms in the United States, representing a top-level product or service. Essentially, when I walked in the front door of an establishment, I looked official. I looked like I belonged.

As a consultant, my professional image expressed to the client that I would communicate a good image to their team once I was hired. From their viewpoint, I was a good role model for how their team should look. It worked. I sold over $35,000 in business the first year I began cold calling, selling products that I had never consulted before.

If image is everything, then it stands to reason you should not scrimp on the image your printed materials project about you either. Every business card, letter or brochure that leaves your office is an extension of you. If you and your printed materials look like a million bucks, that's the kind of money you can potentially make owning your own business. Don't settle for a scruffy image in your printed materials.

Years ago, high-quality graphics and printed materials would have cost thousands of dollars. Now, doing it yourself on a home computer, you can design high-quality materials for zero to a maximum of a hundred dollars. In starting some of my businesses, I've picked up quality envelopes and matching paper from a shop like Kinko's and designed my own graphics right in *WordPerfect*. Instantly, as the laser printer prints, I have generated high-quality corporate identities for the businesses I have owned. Be careful not to select papers that are too generic; they can scream "small business." For a more convincing image, select papers with few preprinted designs on them, more basic in color and high in texture quality.

For a few extra dollars, you can install one of many great desktop publishing packages on your home computer. *Microsoft Publisher* sells for around $100. *PagePlus* is around the same price and comes with extensive graphics and font selections. A more expensive package, *CorelDraw*, comes with a lavish array of fonts, photographs and graphics. If you need something simple, something dedicated just to business cards and stationery, look into packages such as *MySoftwares* and *MyAdvancedBrochures*.

By cutting the cost of hiring a graphic artist, you will have a flexible budget for the printing process. With a good laser printer attached to your home computer, you can also avoid the printing costs of many corporate identity basics like letterhead, envelopes and proposals or contracts. With this strategy, you will save money and still generate the high-quality image you need to look established and successful.

Take action on you and your company's image. Stop a moment and take inventory of your professional image needs. Make a list of the things you will need personally and as a business to communicate the greatest image possible to your customers. If necessary, consider borrowing items or finding other ways to cut costs but still achieve your image goals.

# PROFESSIONAL BUSINESS IMAGE INVENTORY

| Name of Item | Have it | Need it |
|---|---|---|
| 1. Example: Business cards | | x |
| 2. | | |
| 3. | | |
| 4. | | |
| 5. | | |
| 6. | | |
| 7. | | |
| 8. | | |
| 9. | | |
| 10. | | |
| 11. | | |
| 12. | | |
| 13. | | |
| 14. | | |
| 15. | | |

Let's review now what we've learned in this second chapter:

1. If you think you can or can't, in either case you're probably right.
2. Practice positive self-talk.
3. Neutralize negative self-talk with positive winning statements.
4. Take personal responsibility for creating and implementing your own business.
5. Practice visualization.
6. Sell image!

---

| 3 |
|---|

---

# PREPARE A SUCCESSFUL BUSINESS PLAN

When you've never driven somewhere before, perhaps to a new friend's house or to a vacation hideaway, what is the first thing you ask for? You ask for a map or directions. Having a business plan for your own business is exactly that; it's having the directions to somewhere you have never been.

Cheri Fuller, in her book *Home Business Happiness*, states, "It's too easy when you're working from home to not get anything accomplished, to garden or grocery shop." Worse yet, in my opinion, when we fail to plan, we fail to focus on the real meaning and purpose of our business at it relates to profitability and the bottom line. Without a business plan, there is a danger to get sidetracked by your own ideas, others thoughts, and even the competition. With a business plan, Fuller continues, "Your goals are more concrete. And I see if what I'm doing today or this week is leading me toward my goals expressed in the business plan, or if I'm being sidetracked by the urgent. If you've got a plan, you are more likely to meet your goals." In other words, a motto I've heard over and over and always lived by: "Plan your work and work your plan!"

---

**7**

**Write a *simple* business plan. Include just enough information to prompt taking immediate action. Avoid becoming overwhelmed with too much planning and thus paralysis by analysis.**

---

Keep it simple is the message here. There is no need to make your business plan long, wordy and confusing. If it is, you won't follow it, just as you wouldn't follow a map or directions that were written in a tedious and confusing manner. Simplicity guarantees usage. I like to keep my business plans in outline form with basic sub points offering a sound framework. It does not need to be more than three to five pages in length.

As I've mentioned, in conjunction with writing this book, I am starting my seventeenth business out of my home. It has been conceived, developed, refined and launched with the same action plan I am sharing with you in this book. In a moment, I'll share with you its business plan.

One year ago, in Fort Lauderdale, Florida, of all places, I

stepped on ice in hockey skates for the first time in my life. I began taking ice hockey lessons from a professional coach at the official practice facility of the NHL's Florida Panthers. Within eight short months of the first lesson, my coach had prepared me to try out for a position in an amateur league. Being realistic, he also cushioned me for possible disappointment. Long story short, I got picked about halfway through the drafts, became addicted to the sport and became founder and president of the American Hockey Association. What started out as a hobby in less than a year has become a do-what-you-love-to-do business opportunity of a lifetime.

Here is what the business plan looked like when it was first drafted on my computer. Take a look at the key categories addressed in the outline. Observe the sub points. Follow its outline as you construct your own business plan.

## SAMPLE BUSINESS PLAN FORMAT

### The American Hockey Association
### Business Plan First Draft

I. NAME

American Hockey Associations (AHA)

II. VISION

To be the number one prestigious society, offering identity and a sense of belonging to its members; and to be the premier information resource center for hockey enthusiasts.

## III. MISSION

**G**rowth • Grow the sport of hockey among all age groups and at all levels nationwide. Recruit new enthusiasts. Promote it to the masses.

**A**musement • Effectively represent the sport to the nation as great amusement, fun, passion, and develop a genuine love for the sport.

**M**aintain networking • Provide the information necessary for members to form individual and team networks—locally, regionally and nationally.

**E**ducation • Educate members in all aspects of the sport:
Skill training
Safety
Equipment
Conditioning
Nutrition
Coaching
Resources
Information

## IV. PRODUCT DESCRIPTION

Welcome package
Quarterly newsletter
Annual membership directory
Membership card

Logo patch for gear

Accident insurance

## V. COST OF THE PRODUCT

Their cost _____

Our cost   _____

Profit     _____

## VI. SUPPORT STAFF

Newsletter writers

Graphics and logo design artist

Legal advisor

Financial advisor

Internet Web page designer and provider

Administrative assistant

## VII. CAPITAL INVESTMENTS

High-speed laser printer for mailings

Computer for membership and organization management

Software for data base and administration

## VIII. FIRST-YEAR EXPENSES

Monthly Expenses—Telephone, postage, printing, advertising

Capital Expenditures

## IX. FIRST YEAR INCOME

Membership sales _____

Advertising sales  _____

Mailing list sales  _____

## COMPETITION—MARKET RESEARCH

Who in the USA is currently doing something similar?

Who in Canada is doing something similar?

What other membership societies are similar?

What are their fees?

## SALES GOAL

100,000 members a year

## MARKETING PLAN

Internet Web page with instant registration

Print ads in sport magazines

Speaking engagements

Dasher boards at ice and roller rinks

Marketing campaign slogan

"Be Cool Belong"

This plan may seem a bit aggressive to you. Keep in mind, even though I am starting this venture in my home I am clearly committing myself to something larger than a home based business as it grows. You can take the outline of this plan and use it for whatever size business you wish to create and manage. Using this same plan, I've created businesses that were less extensive. They have provided great income and I never had to move the business from my home.

## 8    Choose a descriptive name for the business that creatively says exactly what the business does.

What's in a name? Everything! It is one of the most important decisions you will ever make for your company. In the minds of your customers, your company's name is synonymous with its product.

## PITFALLS TO AVOID WHEN SELECTING A NAME

- Too long with too much to remember
  *Example:* The Vegetarian and Natural Foods Catalog for Health Conscious People
- Doesn't say what you do
  *Example:* a company started out of a home near a lake called the Lakeshore Consulting Group
- Abbreviation or acronym that does not explain the company
  *Example:* a company offering web-site consulting called W.S.C., Inc.
- Too short, not enough information in the name
  *Example:* a company that produces full-color graphic art called Colors, Inc.
- Trendy name that will date the company
  *Example:* a company offering a home and office cleaning service called Three Cleaning Dudes

Now that you know what to avoid in selecting your company's name, here are three steps you can take that will facilitate the creation of the name that is best for your company and product or service:

1. Brainstorm
2. Assemble
3. Finalize

In step one, brainstorm, list below all words and phrases that come to mind in connection with your company's product or service. Creative plays on words are encouraged. Have fun! Don't restrict yourself. Go wild! We will assemble the words later. Incidently, this whole three-step exercise becomes even more fun when you invite friends and family over to be a part of the process.

## BRAINSTORMING YOUR COMPANY'S NAME

List below all words and phrases that come to mind in connection with your company's product or service. Use another sheet of paper if necessary.

_____  _____  _____

_____  _____  _____

_____  _____  _____

_____  _____  _____

_____  _____  _____

_____  _____  _____

_____  _____  _____

_____  _____  _____

_____  _____  _____

_____  _____  _____

_____  _____  _____

In step two, begin to assemble combinations and variations of the words listed in the above exercise. Assemble them into prospective company names. There are no right or wrong answers. Create at least ten name variations using words from the brainstorming list that have some appeal to you, your family and friends. Make sure the names are brief and creative, describe your business and get people's attention.

## ASSEMBLING YOUR COMPANY'S NAME

Create at least ten name variations using words from the brainstorming list that have some appeal to you, your family and friends.

1.

2.

3.

4.

5.

6.

7.

8.

9.

10.

In step three, finalize your company's name. This can take anywhere from a brief moment of inspiration to a few days of reviewing a multitude of combinations from your list in step two. But don't take too long. Usually your first reaction gives you the best name for the business. Again, rely on others' feedback to help solidify the final decision, but you be the final judge.

## FINALIZING YOUR COMPANY'S NAME

Finalize your company's name by selecting one combination of words from step two. Modify, massage and change where necessary, but finalize as soon as possible.

**9** | **Define your vision. That is, answer the questions Why do we exist? What do we want to become in the future?**

In the case of the American Hockey Association, let's take a look at the vision again as defined in its business plan: "To be the number one prestigious society, offering identity and a sense of belonging to its members; and to be the premier information resource center for hockey enthusiasts." In hindsight, does its vision answer the questions Why do we exist? What do we want to become in the future? Yes, clearly it does.

Why is defining your vision so important? Essentially, the vision commits your business to both a short- and long-term objective. With a defined vision there is no wavering. When writing your vision, you need to ensure that every word, every intent is well defined in its statement. Every word must count. Be succinct and to the point.

> **10** Define your vision. That is, answer the questions How am I going to do it? How am I going to get there (to the vision)?

Again, in the case of the American Hockey Association, its mission clearly states how it will become the number one prestigious society and premier resource center for hockey enthusiasts. From its business plan, let's review again its mission, that is, how it will accomplish its vision.

Growth • Grow the sport of hockey among all age groups and at all levels nationwide. Recruit new enthusiasts. Promote it to the masses.

Amusement • Effectively represent the sport to the nation as great amusement, fun, passion, and develop a genuine love for the sport.

**M**aintain networking • Provide the information necessary for members to form individual and team networks—locally, regionally and nationally.

**E**ducation • Educate members in all aspects of the sport:
Skill training
Safety
Equipment
Conditioning
Nutrition
Coaching
Resources
Information

According to C. Davis Fogg, in his book *Team-Based Strategic Planning*, the mission is a navigational star toward which your company aligns its bow in order to reach its desired destination. He states, "Technically, a mission statement's function is to define the business's purpose, direction, and future thrust."

## 11 | Define your product or service.

Basically there are only two kinds of businesses, a product or hard-goods business or a soft, service-oriented business. If you decide to go into a home-based hard-goods business, be sure you can manage it well from a home environment. As we all know, goods take up supply, assembly, and storage space. Examples of this would be pottery, ceramics, canvas art, custom clothing, baked goods and functional crafts. More conducive to a home environment is a service-oriented business. Examples of this would be newsletter writer, publicist, author, wallpaper service, translator, reunion planner, web-page designer and computer consultant. These types of businesses take up little space in comparison to a hard-goods product.

Whatever your decision might be, be sure to take time to define your product or service clearly in your business plan. You now have a blueprint that will help guide you through other issues such as sales, marketing, budget and any necessary capital expenditures to get the business up and running.

In the business plan of the American Hockey Association, was the product or service defined? Yes, it was. The business plan stated that each member would receive the following:

Welcome package
Quarterly newsletter
Annual membership directory
Membership card
Logo patch for gear
Accident insurance
Take time now to define your product or service.

## 12 — Know your costs. Answer the following: What are your costs? What are the client's costs? What is your profit?

Now that you have defined your product, you are better equipped to forecast your costs. Obviously, this is an important part of your business plan. Without it, how would you know what to charge your customers, set budgets and sales goals and determine overall profitability?

Take a moment now to determine your cost per unit. For instance, when I ran the business *YPC*—Your Personal Chef, I determined that my food costs per dining event ran about 50 percent of gross. To fine-dine four people on a five-course meal, my costs ran almost two hundred dollars. I therefore determined the client's cost would be, minimum, one hundred dollars per person or four hundred dollars. It was therefore determined that my profit would be two hundred dollars plus tip. Not bad income for a few hours of work.

## 13 — Define your support staff needs and wages.

The ideal, of course, is to be able to run your company completely solo. Adding labor costs to your business plan is a huge commitment, both financially and emotionally, to the individuals you hire. One company I founded, CareerEdge, grew from a humble beginning on a typewriter in the corner of my bedroom. There were no employees; just me. Within three years we had expanded to a staff of more than ten people. Not only was meeting monthly payroll draining—more than twenty thousand dollars of it—but the various personality types and psychological needs of the employees were, at times, emotionally draining. At one point, I found myself more consumed with employee problems than with what I loved most: talking to customers and running the business.

If you still feel you do need help with running your business, consider using temporary contracted employees. There are many benefits to you when you do this.

## BENEFITS TO HIRING TEMPORARY CONTRACTED EMPLOYEES

- They bring to a key area years of experience that you don't have.
- You avoid related taxes, benefits, training and office overhead.
- Hired consultants are only paid for what they do— you save money.
- You have no long-term commitment to the individual.

- In most cases, they will work harder, knowing they are on contract.

In any case, whether the employee is hired or contracted, you need to plan for their compensation expense in your business plan. Take a moment now and analyze your support staff needs. If you determine there are none, all the better. If you discover some help will be necessary, define their positions and the approximate annual wages for each.

**14**

**Prepare a first-year budget.**
**Estimate numbers for the following:**
- **General operating expenses**
- **Equipment and capital expenditures**
- **Expected wages for support staff**
- **Expected sales**
- **Projected income from all sources**

If you're like me and many entrepreneurs, you score high in the area of creativity, but have low levels of interest in the numbers, financial and analytical side of running a business. The fact of the matter is that budgeting is a necessary evil. Don't make the mistake of ignoring altogether something you don't like, such as budgeting. A successful business has a balanced budget, reflective of total costs against projected sales, and leaving room for a profit as well.

Sometimes being realistic about your expenses may be difficult. One reason being that some entrepreneurs are prone to color the facts. They will omit some expenses from their projections in order to make the company look more viable and profitable than it really is. It's good to be optimistic, but this sort of thinking will come back to haunt you. Also, some individuals have not been self-employed before. They are not totally aware of all the expenses they should be prepared for before launching their business. The following represents a list of expenses you should consider when preparing this part of your business plan. Check off the items on the list that will be of a concern to you. Fill in the estimated monthly and annual expense for each item. Add to the list any expenses unique to your business that are not already listed below.

## DETAILED CHART OF EXPENSES

| Description | Monthly Amount | Annual Amount |
|---|---|---|
| Auto | | |
| Office furniture | | |
| Office equipment | | |
| Advertising | | |
| Bank charges | | |
| Salaries | | |
| Temporary help | | |
| Trade conventions | | |
| Training seminars | | |
| Courier and shipping | | |
| Dues and subscriptions | | |
| Gifts | | |
| Insurance—auto | | |
| Insurance—health | | |
| Insurance—disability | | |
| Insurance—other | | |
| Licenses and permits | | |
| Postage | | |
| Legal | | |
| Tax preparation | | |
| Telephone and beeper | | |
| Travel | | |
| Utilities | | |
| Credit card interest | | |
| Others: | | |
| _____ | | |
| _____ | Total: | Total: |

# 15

## Learn about the competition.

Even though you may have years of experience in the industry in which you are launching your business, take time to learn about the competition. You can learn about your competition through some very basic techniques. For instance, make a phone call to the competitor's office. Request information and and a fee schedule. Or have a friend with an office in an established corporation call a competitor for you. Ask your friend to request information and interview the competitor over the phone. The important thing is to get creative, try different approaches to do your research. As Ed, my sales manager at Lanier Business Systems, always said, "Know thy competition!" Here are the top ten reasons why.

## THE TOP 10 REASONS WHY YOU SHOULD KNOW YOUR COMPETITION

1. To find the weaknesses in their product and make yours better
2. To discover the strengths in their product and benchmark them
3. To learn how to differentiate yourself from the competitors
4. To find out who their customers are

5. To uncover waste in their overhead costs and keep yours lower

6. To get a schedule of their fees and other product costs

7. To gain information about their annual revenues

8. To discover customer opinion of their product or service

9. To be able to sell against them if a customer brings them up

10. To know their history and how long they have been in business

Let's review what we have learned in this third chapter:

7. Write a *simple* business plan.

8. Choose a descriptive name for the business.

9. Define your vision.

10. Define your mission.

11. Define your product or service.

12. Know your costs.

13. Define your support staff needs and wages.

14. Prepare a first-year budget.

15. Learn about the competition.

# DEVELOP LEADS AND A NETWORK

There are numerous stories about individuals who when starting their own businesses had access to a lot of cash to work with. The money usually comes from a life savings or loans. At the outset, these individuals feel secure with their financial nest egg backing them. However, in time fear sets in as days rapidly turn into weeks and weeks into months, expenses mount and the money begins to quickly disappear.

During the start-up phase, many new business owners focus on the office furniture, painting the walls, setting up computers, strategizing, theorizing, socializing, gardening and sometimes even working on their golf or tennis game. In reality, when all is said and done, they have put very little time into the essence of their businesses—that is, networking, lead generation and selling their business. These are the key actions that ultimately translate into profitability. My aunt Florence has a phrase she uses for the times in our lives when we become too financially comfortable. She says we become "fat, dumb and happy." Don't let this happen to you!

How tragic the above scenario is for new business owners. If only they had received the advice here on this page: *Generating leads and networking are the number one activities you need to commit yourself to when becoming a small business owner.* I've italicized that last sentence for emphasis. Read it again. *Generating leads and networking are the number one activities you need to commit yourself to when becoming a small business owner.*

Practically speaking, what does it mean to make these "the number one activities?" To answer that question, I'd like to share the story of a product I launched about ten years ago. It is called Guest*Star.

Guest*Star in its infancy was a training program for hotel and restaurant workers that I designed on my home computer evenings and weekends while I still worked for Lanier Business Systems selling computers. I had known for months that Lanier's computer division in Miami, Florida, was not doing well, and that it was likely I'd be out of a job soon. I had an alternate plan should that day come. I feverishly worked at home to ready the product Guest*Star to sell to the restaurant and hospitality industries beginning the first day I left Lanier.

Upon leaving Lanier, I was ready to hit the ground running. I did not waste precious daytime hours to design a product: it was already done. Now beginning day one I could focus on seeing prospective clients. I did all the preparatory administrative work evenings while I was still employed, a good tip for anyone wanting to transition from employed to self-employed status. Without a dime in savings, I took the start-your-own-business challenge and refused to go out job hunting. I was hungry. I was motivated to see multitudes of prospective clients, make money and lots of it. Within the first sixty days of being unemployed, I sold more than three thousand dollars in Guest*Star seminar business to local establishments. It was not done by sitting at home gardening, theorizing and strategizing. Here's how I did it, and you can do it too by following the same formula.

With a little bit of self-discipline, I awoke each morning no later than 7 A.M. Next came a consistent dedication to do nothing but talk to prospective customers during the hours of 9 to 5. On many days it was more like 8 to 6. All administration, such as client proposals, bookkeeping, mass mailings, filing and the like, was saved for evening and weekend hours when a client could not be seen. As you can see, with administration being tagged onto a full day of sales calls, a typical day would not end until somewhere between 8 and 10 P.M. In some instances, client proposals and mass mailings would consume my hours well past midnight. The strategy worked. Within two years, the business began to remain profitable strictly from referrals. The long days of client meetings and administration began to subside to a more manageable pace.

Realize that in the early phase of any start-up operation, the small business owner needs to face the reality of long hours, seeing hundreds of prospective clients, late nights immersed in administration and, in general, short-term loss for long-term gain.

## 16
Join the $50,000-a-year club!
Secure ten new leads a day for your business; fifty a week.

This success formula requires securing fifty new leads a week that benefit the selling, marketing and promotion of your product or service.

It is an aggressive plan requiring the generation of ten leads a day. In one month, you will have generated a whopping two hundred leads. With this plan placed into action, you are well on your way to joining the $50,000-a-year club.

However, many find this kind of activity difficult. Many come from what I call the cherry-picking school of sales. This is where individuals wait for the leads to come to them. They wait for the phone to ring or someone to knock on their door. Folks, it doesn't work that way in real life. No fairy godmother is going to come along and throw pixie dust and mysteriously make it happen for you. If you are going to be successful at being self-employed, you have to aggressively go out daily, generate leads and make it happen. Denis Waitley, author of *The Psychology of Winning*, states, "Winners make it happen. Losers let it happen."

**17** **Secure twenty contacts a week from cold calls. Simply drop in on twenty businesses or individuals who will benefit from your product or service. Get their names and addresses. Go back home and mail them a marketing letter. Better yet, try to see them while you are there.**

Cold calling, whether you've done it for years or are reading about it here for the first time, is the one thing you must know how to do in order to promote your business.

There are some things people like about it. But most often, there are many things people don't like about it. First, there are the likes: It gets you out of the house, meeting and socializing with others, which can be a welcome and refreshing activity in the life of any homebound small business owner. Cold calling, no doubt about it, generates customers and money. This is definitely a welcome outcome for someone who needs to pay the bills.

But what about the dislikes of cold calling? There are many aspects of it that make it downright tough. The first, in one word: *rejection*! In an average day, depending on your product or service, you can make five, ten, even twenty cold calls. Out of say twenty, you may get to see five people. Out of those five, if you have an excellent presentation, you'll acquire at least one hot lead. Most people have trouble with the nineteen no's that it takes to get to the one hot lead. In fact, in cold calling, loving rejection, loving the word "no" is part of the territory. For every no you get, you are one step closer to a yes. The second thing people dislike about cold calling is that it needs to be done on almost a daily basis. You have to be out there every day. If you're not, then your competition will be. It is my firm belief you don't need an advertising budget for most businesses you may start. Save the money. You are the advertising when you go out on a consistent basis, network and sell your business.

While you are on a cold call, request from the receptionist the business card of the decision maker who contracts people in your area of expertise. If you don't see the decision maker while you are there, return home and mail him or her a marketing letter and your business card.

Some may think I'm crazy! I'm not. You no longer can excuse yourself from the hard work of learning how to cold call. For any business owner, getting out of your comfort zone, meeting strangers, learning to think on your feet and spontaneously selling your company are imperative.

In the first two years that I sold the customer service training product Guest*Star, cold calls were made to every major hotel and restaurant from Key West through to Miami, Fort Lauderdale and Orlando, Florida. No stone was left unturned. The result: a very successful customer service system that to this very day, ten years later, is used all around the country, now strictly on a referral basis. It is still making money and still going strong. But it is more sophisticated than it was and quite evolved from its beginnings, though it still retains its roots.

The following is a script developed especially to help you become familiar with the anatomy of a cold call. Roleplay it with a friend. Within a few practice sessions, you'll be ready to go out and begin promoting your own product or service.

## COLD-CALLING SCRIPT WITH FULL COOPERATION

BUSINESS OWNER *(to the receptionist)*: Good morning/afternoon, my name is ————. I would like to speak to the person who is responsible for the area of ———— (e.g. publicity, computers, marketing, etc.). Who would that be?

RECEPTIONIST: That is Ms./Mr. ————. What is this in regard to?

BUSINESS OWNER: Please let Ms./Mr. ———— know I stopped by to discuss ————. *(Stop talking. Don't give any more information than is necessary.)*

RECEPTIONIST: Can you be more specific?

BUSINESS OWNER: Just let him/her know that I'm here to discuss ————. *(Again stop talking. Limit the amount of information you give.)*

RECEPTIONIST: Please wait one moment. *(She dials the phone)*. If you would, please be seated. Ms./Mr. ———— will be out in a moment to see you.

BUSINESS OWNER: Thank you for all your help.
Your name is? Thank you,————, for everything.

*(When the person in charge comes out to lobby, proceed to ask one or two key questions to gather information about that person's area. Next, suggest a quiet spot where you could share with him/her how you can help the company and assist them in increasing quality, reducing costs and time, etc. Before leaving, request another appointment to present a proposal. Get a business card.)*

## COLD-CALLING SCRIPT WITH A CHALLENGE

BUSINESS OWNER: *(To the receptionist)*: Good morning/afternoon, my name is ———. I would like to speak to the person who is responsible for the area of ——— (e.g. publicity, computers, marketing, etc.). Who would that be?

RECEPTIONIST: That is Ms./Mr ———. What is this in regard to?

BUSINESS OWNER: Please let Ms./Mr ——— know I stopped by to discuss ———. *(Stop talking. Don't give any more information than is necessary.)*

RECEPTIONIST: Can you be more specific?

BUSINESS OWNER: Just let him/her know that I'm here to discuss ———. *(Again stop talking. Limit the amount of information you give.)*

RECEPTIONIST: Please wait one moment. *(She dials the phone.)* I'm sorry. Ms./Mr. ——— cannot see you right now.

BUSINESS OWNER: I completely understand. May I have a business card for Ms./Mr. ——— or one for the company? *(Receptionist hands business owner the business card.)* Thank you for all your help. Your name is? Thank you, ———, for everything.

*(Business owner exits and writes down the receptionist's name and other pertinent notes in a notebook before going on to the next call.)*

## COLD CALLING TIPS

- Attack at dawn! You've got a whole hour before 9 A.M. when the key decision maker is available without a secretary to screen calls and appointments.
- Attack at dusk! Same principle. You've got a whole hour after 5 P.M. when the key decision maker is available without a secretary to screen calls and appointments.
- Make friends with secretaries. Make them allies and not adversaries. One way to do this is to remember the secretary's name and to use it.
- Refrain from giving the secretary too much information. Give just enough to prompt a visit from the boss.
- Avoid closed-ended questions, such as "Is Mr. Robinson in? Is he available to be seen for a moment?" The answer is, of course, "No." Be direct. An example would be "Please let Mr. Robinson know I am here to discuss the company's computer network."

**18** Secure twenty contacts a week from calling businesses listed in directories such as the Yellow Pages, the Chamber of Commerce and association lists. Send them a marketing letter and business card after your call.

The same process of cold calling I just described to you can be adapted for marketing your company by telephone.

One product and company I founded, under the name CareerEdge, was quite conducive to promoting by telephone. CareerEdge specialized in promoting job fairs and career seminars nationwide.

The sales goal of CareerEdge job fairs was to have up to one hundred companies participate in the job fairs by purchasing booth space for between $400 and $800 per space, per fair. What lists would you work from in order to promote CareerEdge by telephone? Think a moment. What did you come up with?

Here's how we did it. One resource that was extremely productive was the Sunday edition of the particular city's help wanted ads. We felt that if a company was advertising for employees, then a job fair would also be appealing to them. It was my job to go through the paper every Sunday evening and circle companies that I would begin calling Monday morning. CareerEdge was also promoted over the phone by using copies of each city's Yellow Page directory. The directory was obtained quite easily by visiting the main library or by getting a copy from a friend that lived in that particular city. It was a great source of leads for vertical markets that we knew were predisposed to utilizing job fairs. Further, we worked from Chamber of Commerce lists as well as directories published for key industries, such as the hospitality or restaurant industries. The number of available lists for networking, promotion and lead generation was so great, it was humanly impossible to call all the leads.

To help prepare you for utilizing the telephone to promote your company and its product or service, I've created a telemarketing script for you. As with the cold calling script, practice with a friend or family member. The more you do it, the easier it becomes.

## TELEMARKETING SCRIPT WITH FULL COOPERATION

BUSINESS OWNER *(to the switchboard operator)*: Good morning/afternoon, my name is ———. I would like to speak to the person who is responsible for the area of ——— (e.g. publicity, computers, marketing, etc.). Who would that be?

SWITCHBOARD OPERATOR: Yes, that is Ms./Mr. ——— . Please hold while I transfer you.

*(Business owner is transferred.)*

SECRETARY: Good morning/afternoon. Ms./Mr. ———'s office.

BUSINESS OWNER *(sounding confident)*: Good morning/afternoon, this is ——— calling. Ms./Mr. ———, please.

SECRETARY: What is this in regards to?

BUSINESS OWNER: Please let Ms./Mr. ——— know I'm calling to discuss ———. *(Stop talking. Don't give any more information than is necessary.)*

SECRETARY: Please hold one moment. Ms./Mr. ——— will be with you shortly.

BUSINESS OWNER: Thank you very much. I'll hold.

*(When the person in charge comes on the phone, introduce your-self and briefly your product or service. Next, ask one or two key open-ended questions to gather information about the company's needs. The goal of the phone call is to set up an appointment. Before hanging up, request an appointment time or even offer to take the person to lunch. Get the correct spelling of his or her name, company and address.)*

## TELEMARKETING SCRIPT WITH A CHALLENGE

BUSINESS OWNER *(to the switchboard operator)*: Good morn-ing/afternoon, my name is ———. I would like to speak to the person who is responsible for the area of ——— (e.g. publicity, computers, marketing, etc.). Who would that be?

SWITCHBOARD OPERATOR: Yes, that is Ms./Mr. ———. Please hold while I transfer you. *(Business owner is transferred.)*

SECRETARY: Good morning/afternoon. Ms./Mr. ———'s office.

BUSINESS OWNER *(sounding confident)*: Good morning/after-noon, this is ——— calling. Ms./Mr. ———, please.

SECRETARY: What is this in regards to?

BUSINESS OWNER: Please let Ms./Mr. ——— know I'm

calling to discuss ———. *(Stop talking. Don't give any more information than is necessary.)*

SECRETARY: Please hold one moment. *(She places the business owner on hold.)* I'm sorry, Ms./Mr. ——— is not available.

BUSINESS OWNER *(being politely insistent):* It's very important that I speak with him/her. I can hold a moment more and see if he/she frees up.

SECRETARY: I'm sorry. he/she is very busy right now.

BUSINESS OWNER: I understand. What would be a better time to try back? Later this morning, or this afternoon?

SECRETARY: Probably this afternoon.

BUSINESS OWNER: I'm sending Ms./Mr. ———some important information. How do you spell their name and what is the address, please? *(The secretary provides the information.)* Thank you very much for all your help. Your name is? Thank you, ———, for everything.

*(The business owner hangs up the phone and mails a business card and marketing letter to the key person. A day or two after the information arrives, the business owner calls back, remembers to use the secretary's name and gets transferred to the person to whom the information was mailed.)*

In my book *Get the Job You Want in Thirty Days,* I give anyone cold calling and encountering secretaries some important advice: "Highly efficient secretaries are probably the biggest obstacle when cold calling or telemarketing. Please understand that they are only doing their job. Be polite and do not take it personally. However, there are ways to encourage cooperation from a secretary. One way is to sound assumptive and authoritative. If you sound important and professional (not weak or scared) in many instances you will be put right through to the manager, no questions asked. Also, you can call before or after business hours. At this time the secretary is gone and the manager usually answers the phone. I have had tremendous cooperation from switchboard operators. Call the operator and ask authoritatively, 'What's that extension for Ms./Mr.'s office?' or ask, 'What is the direct dial phone number for Ms./Mr.'s office?' Sound like you work in the building and you lost their number. It works. Get the extension, call back in, and simply ask for the number you were given."

Also, in that same book it is explained that you should take care not to give too much information when calling companies and their departments: "What do you do if they ask you to leave your name and number? Don't! If you leave your name and number, they've got you. Everyone knows not to put you through when you call back. It could hinder future return calls and getting secretarial cooperation. To avoid leaving my name and number, I usually say, 'Oh, no, that's okay. I'm between appointments right now. I can call back later. What would be the best time to try back?'

## 19. Secure ten leads a week through networking. Attend business association meetings, community organizations and functions.

Owning your own business means getting out and meeting people. Staying at home and having a love affair with your computer and T.V. is not going to help promote your business. You need to get out on a weekly basis. Think of yourself as a politician out on a campaign, in your case a very long one. Your sole responsibility is to promote yourself.

Tom started his own small private law practice in Fort Lauderdale after observing widespread layoffs at a major telecommunications company in South Florida where he worked as an international major accounts manager. "I had close friends terminated. I watched more than twenty people I worked with over the course of a year terminated. As I watched this, it caused me to consider something else for my life. As a result, I became more inspired to open my own business."

Within a few weeks of launching his small venture, he was overwhelmed with the volume of business he had generated through networking. How did he go from zero to thousands of dollars in income in less than a month? Here is a small list of the many associations he joined and positions he held in order to shake hands, hand out business cards and just let people know he was there.

## TOM'S SUCCESS RECIPE FOR COMMUNITY INVOLVEMENT AND NETWORKING

- University of Florida Gold Coast Gator Club President
- Palm Beach County Fair Housing/Employment Board
- Task Force on Quality and Equality of Education
- American Red Cross co-chairperson of Fund Raising
- American Alzheimer's Association fund raising chair
- Ambassadors Council of Tower Club
- Political and civic associations
- International Business Advisory Council of Chamber
- Member of conduct committee on local politics

Tom's list is just a small sample of the many unique networking opportunities that exist. There are many professional associations that relate to your business, directly or indirectly, and they usually meet monthly. You may or may not know about them. Do some research, then go out there and start promoting yourself and your business. It works. Just ask Tom and thousands like him who have achieved success through the art of networking.

## NETWORKING RESOURCES

Here is an expanded list of creative resources for networking.

- Professional associations
- Country clubs
- Health clubs
- Organized league sports such as golf, tennis, bowling, hockey, etc.
- Special interest chat rooms on-line
- Former colleagues and coworkers
- Clergy
- Former teachers
- Political associations
- Religious organizations
- Charitable fund-raising organizations
- Church functions
- Clubs for special hobbies and interests
- Professionals such as your doctor, lawyer, banker, etc.
- Business travelers, airports and airplanes
- After-work pubs, clubs and restaurants for business professionals
- Chambers of Commerce

**20**

> Develop leads relentlessly—daily from 9 to 5 (if you are still at another job, on evenings and weekends)—until you achieve your sales goal. Do not waste business hours writing proposals, book-keeping or even washing your car.

Essentially, in almost any businesses that one might own, the hours of 9 to 5 are the magic hours of networking and lead generation. There is practically no other time for the bulk of these activities. As you can imagine, there will always be temptations to lure the business owner away from the hard task of developing leads for his or her business. For instance, I hear comments all the time from friends who know I am self-employed. Their concern is that if they were self-employed, they would find it difficult to get up in the morning, they would probably watch TV most of the day and generally find it difficult to get motivated. When you're hungry, literally, and have to pay the bills, you will be motivated to accomplish the daily activities that effectively promote your business.

One small business owner reserved the necessary funds to get out and promote her business by lowering the thermostat in the winter and living on a low-cost diet of beans and peanut butter and jelly sandwiches for the entire first year of operation. In her second year, she became extremely profitable. Her hard work and sacrifices paid off. Yours will too if you follow a similar formula of dedication to promoting your business on a daily basis.

Let's review what we have learned in this fourth chapter:

16. Secure ten new leads a day for your business; fifty a week.
17. Secure twenty contacts a week from cold calls.
18. Secure an additional twenty contacts a week from calling businesses listed in directories.
19. Secure ten leads a week through networking.
20. Develop leads relentlessly—daily from 9 to 5.

# SELL YOU AND YOUR BUSINESS

After you have performed all the necessary networking and lead generation activities, the next step is to sell your product to the prospects you have contacted. Good selling skills are synonymous with good communication. If the customer does not buy, in most cases it is because you have not communicated effectively the benefits of your product or service.

Many fear selling. In *Get the Job You Want in Thirty Days*, I state, "The word *selling* creates hesitation and fear in many people. Possibly you are one of them. You may have memories of yourself as a schoolchild selling candy bars door-to-door. You may subconsciously relive the rejection and the slammed doors at the mere thought of selling.

"For others, the idea of selling may conjure up thoughts of

men in plaid suits selling used cars that they know don't work." As a result of these negative images, the idea of selling you and your business is repulsive and not something you would ever care to do. Reassessing one's attitude toward selling is essential to become successful at owning your own business.

To succeed, a business owner must communicate his or her product or service by wearing what I call "the five hats of effective selling." In our current competitive business environment, sales is more than writing up orders and playing golf or tennis at the local country club. Sorry. Success is determined by how well you build trust with a client by wearing the following hats when you are communicating with them.

## THE FIVE HATS OF EFFECTIVE SELLING

These five hats you wear every time you encounter a prospect or customer.

### FRIEND

People buy from people they like. That's just the way it is. We don't go back to restaurants where we did not like the employees; we don't go back to hotels and other establishments where the people were not friendly. People buy from people they like. You and I are no different.

Getting the customer to like you and becoming the customer's friend is the first step in establishing trust with him or her. If the prospect likes you, then he or she will trust you enough to buy from you. Establishing an immediate liking and friendship unconsciously obligates the other person to want to do business with you.

In our hurried and fast-paced world, many find it difficult to take a few extra quality moments to build effective long-term relationships that last with our business prospects and clients. But if done properly, it is time well spent. Here is my top ten list for establishing good friendships and relationships with those to whom you are selling your product or service.

## TOP 10 WAYS TO QUICKLY BUILD FRIENDSHIPS WITH CUSTOMERS

1. *Use and remember their name.* Use the name at least once or twice per encounter. If you don't know someone's name, ask. It is that simple.

2. *Use your name.* Take the initiative and introduce yourself to others.

3. *Go the extra mile.* Deliver more than what the person expected. In essence, exceed expectations.

4. *Smile.* People who smile are considered likable and credible.

5. *Use an icebreaker.* Don't always talk about business. Talk about things not related to business. If you're feeling uncreative, the weather always works.

6. *Offer a sincere compliment.*

7. *Send notes.* Send them for birthdays, anniversaries, congratulations and for many other reasons. People like to be remembered and they will remember you by giving you their business.

8. *Give gifts.* Don't be cheap. Even if you have to charge it, do it. Prospects and customers appreciate gifts and will give you their business when you remember them with small tokens of friendship.

9. *Return phone calls immediately.*

10. *Be negotiable and flexible.* When dealing with prospects and customers, work with them. They will be loyal to you and become lifelong customers.

## CONSULTANT

Take a consultative approach when selling to a prospect or customer. No one likes the hard-sell fast-talker approach. A good consultant takes time in his or her sales presentation to learn about the customer's needs before speaking up and selling his or her business. Here is a sample dialogue between a prospective customer and a business owner speaking in a consultative manner on the prospects turf.

## CONSULTATIVE SELLING DIALOGUE

BUSINESS OWNER *(to the prospect once the initial friendship stage has been established)*: Before we get started, what are some of the things you would like to accomplish in our time together today? Let's set an agenda. This way, we can be sure to address your questions, issues and concerns.

PROSPECT: That is a great idea. Actually, I would like to allow us enough time to give you an overview of our company and to find out more about exactly what it is that you do and how you can help us.

BUSINESS OWNER: I understand. A good plan then would be to take a few moments now to get an overview of your company, possibly even a brief tour, and then I have some questions I've prepared to ask in order to learn more about your particular needs.

PROSPECT: Yes, that would be fine, we can do that now.

*(The business owner and prospect complete the tour and the discovery of the prospect's needs.)*

BUSINESS OWNER: Now that I understand your needs better, let me share some information about my company . I can briefly discuss our history, our customers, and some ideas and solutions that I would like to suggest as an initial way to help you and your company.

*(The business owner proceeds to discuss the background of his/her company and suggests various possible ideas and solutions to the prospect based on his/her needs.)*

PROSPECT: I see. Well, we can really use your help. How much is this going to cost me?

BUSINESS OWNER: I am very flexible and tailor costs to the size of a business as well as the scope of a project. What I would like to suggest, is for me to create a proposal with some ideas and solutions for your situation based on today's meeting. Next, in that proposal there will be some initial investment numbers that we can finalize later depending on the scope of the project we agree on. I'll have that proposal sent to you express mail within a couple of days.

PROSPECT: Thank you for all your help. I'll look forward to hearing back from you real soon.

What did you like about the script? How was it a consultative approach? How does this dialogue differ from the fast-talking hard-sell approach? If someone was selling you a product or service, which approach would you prefer?

It is clear that this script works for a number of reasons. First, the business owner begins the consultation by asking the prospect to set the expectations for the meeting. The prospect is in control. Secondly, the business owner's next step is to learn about the prospect and his or her needs. This is called *solution selling*. It is the process of learning about another's needs, then translating what you have into a solution to their perceived needs. Lastly, this is a good dialogue because the focus is left on the solution and not on money. The issue of money is deferred until a comprehensive proposal has been discussed. This approach gives the prospect complete control over the number of dollars invested when he or she finalizes the scope of the proposal.

Although this dialogue has been written for a product or service being sold to a prospect in a company office environment, its consultative approach is transferrable to any type of selling situation you and your business may encounter. Solution selling, the consultative approach, remains the same.

## DOCTOR

When selling face-to-face to your customer or prospect, realize that he or she is the patient and you are the doctor. Conventional wisdom has it that "People don't care how much you know until they know how much you care."

The relationship of doctor-patient, according to Tom Hopkins, the author of *How to Master the Art of Selling* is best described as "make them sick—make them well." What is meant by this?" In essence, it refers to the process by which a buyer is led to feel the pain of his or her current condition while being without your product or service. Your job is one of being sympathetic to this plight and to make the buyer well with what you have to offer.

Trying to explain this further could be *excessively burdensome* and may make it more complex than it really is. (There, I just made you sick!) Here is some sample dialogue to *make it easier for you to understand* (There, I just made you well!) by actually showing you how to make prospects sick and then how to make them well.

## THE DOCTOR'S MAKE-THEM-SICK AND MAKE-THEM-WELL DIALOGUE

BUSINESS OWNER *(to the prospect once the initial consultative discovery stage has been established)*: You mentioned earlier that you and your employees have been putting *enormous* numbers of hours into meeting what seem to be *impossible* deadlines for many months now. Not only are your consistently long work hours *tiresome,* but overtime can *lower department morale.* I would imagine the amount of overtime hours are very *costly* as well.

PROSPECT: It's been very difficult keeping employee morale high under the circumstances. Also it's taking a toll on my home life. In fact, I think my spouse is getting ready to divorce me if I don't start arriving home at a decent hour.

BUSINESS OWNER: I understand. One of the reasons why companies like yourself engage my consulting services is that I have the time to strictly focus on your issues. As you'll see detailed in my proposal, I'll be taking full responsibility for the many areas that are currently eroding your workday. Because of my years of expertise in projects like yours, I'll be able to save you both time and money. In fact, once I get on board, you may even get some extra time at home. Surely your family will love you for that.

PROSPECT *(laughing):* Sounds good to me. When can you start?

In the first paragraph of this script, the business owner capitalizes on something painful the prospect said earlier. In the business owner's dialogue, the pain words are *italicized*. These are the words that make the prospect sick. As you can see, in the remainder of the dialogue the business owner selectively chooses words that make the prospect well. You can be the doctor and utilize this type of communication at any point in any customer encounter.

## PROBLEM SOLVER

As a small business owner, I not only sell my products and services to others, but I hire other small business owners from time to time to help me achieve my business goals. For instance, my attorney and CPA, coincidentally both named Tom, own small private practices in the Fort Lauderdale area. I am fortunate to have found two individuals who have my loyalty and business because they have the unique ability to assess my situation and solve my problems in a professional manner.

My problems are unique, and they recognize it and work with me by taking responsibility for solving them. For instance, as a writer, author, speaker, consultant and entrepreneur I spend little time at home, so they keep meetings with me to a minimum and take full responsibility for solving my problems.

It has been their problem-solving approach that has kept me engaging their services. They are obviously not the only attorney and CPA in Fort Lauderdale, but they are for me. They are the only two professionals that I have found that take full responsibility for my problems and issues, and solve them while being sensitive to my unique needs.

To build a successful word-of-mouth business, be a problem solver. Take full responsibility for your prospects' and customers' problems and issues. Let them know you care by accommodating their unique needs. Tailor your services to their problems, not to what is convenient for you to give or do.

## PROFESSIONAL PARTNER

I heard a story recently from a friend at Penn State University that illustrates the true essence of professional partnerships. As the story goes, a gentleman owning a farm seemed to have an awkward, ongoing problem with his neighbors, one on either side of his farmhouse: his cows had a propensity for wandering through holes in his fence and onto both neighbors' property.

The neighbor to the right of him was kind enough to knock on his door one day and say, "Your cows have wandered onto my land, but I have returned them and they are now safely on your side of the fence." Of course the farmer thanked him for his kindness. However, not much time had passed before there was a knock on the door and the neighbor to the left of him said, "Your cows have wandered onto my land and I have returned them. Also, I just wanted to let you know that it was no problem, but my son and I have repaired the hole in the fence where the cows wandered through."

Which neighbor was just a friend? Which neighbor was

a partner? Although a simple story, it is quite powerful in illustrating the importance of forming partnerships when it comes to selling your company's product or service. Like the first neighbor, you can choose to just deliver the goods, or like the second neighbor, you can choose to build a partnership, a relationship that will last forever. Do it by going above and beyond your customer's expectations.

## ASK FOR THE CUSTOMER'S BUSINESS

Wearing all five hats perfectly, as just described, still does not guarantee you the sale. It is also critical that you know how to ask or close for the customer's business. Here are five power closes that you can use to help finalize and clinch the deal.

## FIVE POWER CLOSES

1. *The Alternate Close.* Ask an either/or question. Example: "When would you prefer to start the project? Would it be best this month or next month? *(When the prospect answers the question, you know you have the sale.)*

2. *The Misinformed Close.* Ask a question that requires the prospect's correction. Example: "Did you say the low season for your business is summer and we can start the project at that time?" Of course you knew the low season was winter, but the prospect's correcting you will involve him or her in the buying process.

3. *The Minor-Point Close.* Ask a question secondary to

asking for the prospect's business. Example: "How many managers do you plan on assigning to work with me on this project?" When the prospect answers this question, you have him or her already committing to giving you business.

4. *The Assumptive Close.* Make an assumptive closing statement. Example: "I'll go ahead and check into flight schedules and fares and make sure we get the best deal possible to keep my travel expenditures to a minimum." When being assumptive, such as this example demonstrates, you are easing yourself into the desired result without the individual having to make a yes or no decision.

5. *The Creating-Urgency Close.* Make statements that make it urgent that the prospect employs your services as soon as possible. Example: "How soon can we finalize working together? At this time of year my schedule can get booked quite rapidly and we should go ahead and reserve the days that would be most preferable to you in order to accommodate your needs." By creating urgency in your closing statements, you send a strong message to the prospect that you are in demand.

**21** When selling your product or service, there are only two ways to learn about a customer's needs. Listen and ask good open-ended questions.

A person who listens well and asks open-ended questions is perceived as more intelligent than one who doesn't. Listening is the first effective tool we have in our arsenal to effectively learn about our customers' needs. Listening sounds easy, but it is one of the most difficult skills to master. Consider that research has shown that in the communication process, we retain roughly 20 to 40 percent of what we hear. But why aren't we getting the rest of the information?

There are many barriers to good listening. We should become aware of them and avoid them when interacting with prospects and customers. Keep the barriers in mind the next time you are communicating with someone. Once you become aware of them you will be able to control their dangerous affects.

## BARRIERS TO EFFECTIVE LISTENING

- Lack of sleep
- Lack of nutrition
- Distracted by the speaker's voice
- Distracted by something about the speaker's image
- Lack of time
- Think you know it all
- Wishing you were somewhere else
- Anticipating what you think the speaker is going to say
- Thinking about what you are going to say
- Prejudgement and preconceived ideas about the speaker

- Impatience
- Laziness
- Selective hearing: only taking in what you want to hear

Overcoming bad listening skills pays off in big benefits. When you counteract poor listening skills, you gain the ability to gather information, which in turn gives you power to influence and sell the customer. Effective listeners realize they can gain much more by listening than by doing all the talking.

So go ahead and try various listening techniques on your friends, family and customers in order to sharpen your listening skills. You'll be glad you did. Here are some effective listening techniques to help you improve at being a good listener.

## EFFECTIVE LISTENING TECHNIQUES

- Maintain eye contact, but don't stare either.
- Lean forward a bit if sitting in a chair.
- Take occasional subtle but deep breaths.
- Take short notes when possible.
- Nod your head and use other appropriate body language.
- Ask to go to a quieter area if there are distractions in the room.
- Turn your pager and cellular phone off.

The second way to gather information about your customer or prospect is through the art of asking good open-ended questions. Why open-ended questions? This type of question provides you, the seller, with more information than more routine yes-and-no-type questions. Open-ended questions are formed with who, what, where, when, how and why.

For instance, an ineffective question, a close-ended question, would be "Does your department use consultants?" Whether they do or don't, the best answer is no. It's quick, it's easy and gets rid of you and the conversation quite quickly. As a seller, a close-ended question is a sure way to bring your sales call to an abrupt end.

## CLOSE-ENDED QUESTIONS

Is
Are
Were
Have
Am
Has
Will
Do
Does
Can
Would

Conversely, an effective open-ended question would be "What are the current projects you are working on in your department? How are the responsibilities divided up among the team members?" These questions create dialogue. The also create an atmosphere of gathering and exchanging information. It is information that you will use later to sell the customer.

## OPEN-ENDED QUESTIONS

Who
What
Where
When
How
Why
Tell me about…
Please explain to me…
Define for me…

Take the following close-ended questions and write out what you think would be better, more effective open-ended questions.

## OPEN-ENDED QUESTION
## PRACTICE SHEET

1. Closed: "Are you looking to expand?"

   Open:

2. Closed: "Do you ever use consultants?"

   Open:

3. Closed: "Is everything okay with your current supplier?"

   Open:

4. Closed: "Will you consider my services for the project?"

   Open:

5. Closed: "Do you ever find errors by the person you currently use?"

   Open:

6. Closed: "Can I help you?"

   Open:

The night before your prospect or customer presentation prepare your wardrobe and yourself. By now you should have researched the company you are planning to visit. Make sure you have done your homework! Prepare a list of questions you will ask at the sales presentation. Having a list of good, well-thought-out questions makes you appear both professional and competent. These are qualities that ultimately sell your product and services.

In this next exercise, narrow down a list of ten good questions that you will ask during most customer selling situations you will encounter. This list will become the basis of all questions you will ask at your upcoming sales presentations.

## QUESTIONS YOU WILL ASK
## PROSPECTS AND CUSTOMERS

1.

2.

3.

4.

5.

6.

7.

8.

9.

10.

**22** Use role-plays to practice for a customer presentation the night before. Ask a friend to play the role of the customer.

An actor would never dream of going on stage without practicing. His or her performance would be destined to fail without adequate rehearsal.

Although most business professionals agree that practicing their sales presentation is a good idea, more often than not, people tell me they do not practice at all. What a tragedy. The lack of practice can be directly correlated to a lack of sales.

When I first started to train to be an ice hockey player, I was practicing once a week. Then after a few months at this pace, my coach explained to me that if I wanted to be really good, I would have to practice more. At his suggestion, I began to practice three days a week. You know what? He was right. Practice paid off. I was soon achieving excellence of performance that people who'd been playing the sport for years still had not achieved. Practice puts you a cut above the competition. I've learned that both on and off the ice.

So why don't we practice when we know we should? Here are the top 10 reasons others have told me why they do not practice the night before a customer presentation. By becoming aware of them, we have the power to change our attitude and begin to do what's right for our business.

## THE TOP 10 REASONS WHY WE DON'T LIKE TO PRACTICE

1. Don't have time
2. No one to practice with
3. Think its stupid
4. Wouldn't know where to begin
5. Feel awkward doing it with a friend
6. Would rather wing it with the customer
7. Overly self-confident
8. No place quiet to go to do it
9. Don't have an organized presentation prepared
10. Wish experts like me would quit bugging them to practice

Now that you are aware of why you don't like to practice, you are ready to do it. Before your friend or family member arrives to help you, make the following preparations:

1. List the questions you will ask the customer to discover his or her needs.
2. List the anticipated questions you think the customer will ask you.
3. List the top objections you think the customer will have about your product or service.
4. Review the five hats to wear when selling a customer beginning on page 80.

When the person arrives who is going to play the role of the customer, give him or her background on the type of company or situation you will be selling in. Further, give your partner instruction as to the character and personality type of the person(s) you will be making your presentation to. Hand him or her a list of questions you anticipate being asked, so that your partner can drill you.

Have fun and make mistakes. Who cares? It's better to feel awkward now than when you are making the presentation. Role-play a minimum of two to four hours the night before a customer presentation.

> # 23
> **Arrive at an appointment at least ten minutes early. If you arrive on time, you're late.**

As the key representative of your company's product or service, it is imperative that you make an excellent first impression. One way to do this is to arrive at all of your appointments ten minutes early. Arriving any earlier than this could be an inconvenience and should be avoided. Arriving late makes a bad first impression. You never get a second chance to make a first impression.

Arriving early places you in a state of mind that is relaxed and not hurried. It sets the right pace for the customer encounter. Secondly, you provide yourself time to observe the company and gather valuable information about them. Also, while waiting, you can rehearse in your mind the exact presentation performance you role-played the night before.

In the book *Get the Job You Want in Thirty Days*, there is a section that explains the do's and don'ts of waiting in the reception area. Let's review that list for a brief moment again now.

## THE DO'S AND DONT'S OF
## WAITING IN THE RECEPTION AREA

- Do sit professionally while waiting.
- Don't read magazines or newspapers to pass the time.
- Do review your prepared questions and notes.
- Do rehearse in your mind the customer presentation.

**24**

**Do not discuss costs at the beginning of a presentation. Build value first.**

**Discuss general costs in the last few minutes of a presentation. Send detailed costs later in the form of a proposal or contract.**

Just a few days ago I was presenting to a prospect my customer service training system Guest*Star. I was not in his office a minute and already he began with "How much is this going to cost me?" In fact, the prospect was so cost sensitive, he had also asked me to quote prices over the phone before I ever made it to his office for the sales call.

This is not an unusual case. It is actually more the norm. But what do you do? Do you go ahead and immediately start talking money before you've had a chance to introduce your product? Should you quote a price before you've had a chance to build value and understand the scope of the customer's needs? Of course the answer to all of these questions is, no.

In the situation just mentioned, avoid discussing exact numbers both on the phone and at the outset of the sales presentation. While on the phone, simply say, "There is a broad range of costs involved, depending on the scope of your needs. Once we get together and talk, we will be able to narrow that for you."

At the outset of a customer's presentation the time is still not right to discuss money. If the customer presses you for an answer, you can possibly say, "I understand your concern. Once we've had an opportunity to talk and you learn more about what it is I can do for you, and I understand your needs better, we should be able to negotiate a total investment that will work well within your budget."

Of course you know the reasoning behind this approach. If you state a figure that is too high before you've had a chance to build value, you will put yourself way out of the ballpark and the customer will tune you out for the whole rest of the presentation. If you state a figure that is too low, you'll be perceived as cheap and unreliable.

Discussion of total costs should come at the end of your presentation. In a situation where I'm selling my customer service training program Guest*Star, I continue to give rough estimates to the very end of the presentation. I never commit in the presentation because I need time to look at all the variables. I let the prospect know that I will work up a complete proposal and have the exact numbers and scope of the project to them by express mail within two or three days. I have found this approach to be consistently satisfying to customers.

And don't worry if while in your presentation the customer has an objection. I love objections. Truly! Because to me that means the prospect is thinking. Objections tell me the lights are on and someone has been listening to me. The customers that worry me the most are the quiet ones. They are the ones that sit there with a blank stare and nod their head yes the whole time. This person is not going to buy your product or service. Only the person with an objection truly has the right qualifications to buy from you.

Here is a sales formula for handling objections. It is called, Feel, Felt, Found. Let's use it on an actual objection. At my customer's Guest*Star presentation the other day, he stated the following objection: "We don't have a large enough Human Resource Department to manage a comprehensive customer service training program like Guest*Star."

Now let's go ahead and handle his objection with our formula. First, Feel. "I understand how you feel." Second, Felt. "In fact, my client Vacation Hotels, International felt the same way." Third, Found. "And you know what? They found that they had great success with Guest*Star by training department managers to run the training program. By getting the managers involved, they found it to be a greater overall benefit to the organization than if it would have been managed by the Human Resource Department."

In other words, let them know you understand how they Feel. Let the prospect know that others you have worked with have Felt the same way. Finally, let the person know what your other customers Found to be the solution to their objection. It means much more to the customer if another customer solved the objection than if you try to handle the objection with your own opinion.

In summary, a customer presentation is purely a selling situation. The one who practices and utilizes the best tried and proven selling skills wins. Remember, ultimately the customer is buying you, more than your product or service. So always keep in mind that no matter how many customer encounters you have, ultimately you are the greatest product you will ever sell and the customer will ever buy.

Let's review now what we've learned in this chapter:

21. Listen and ask good open-ended questions.
22. Use role-plays with a friend to practice for a customer presentation the night before.
23. Arrive at an appointment at least ten minutes early.
24. Do not discuss costs at the beginning of a presentation. Build value first.

---

6

---

# FOLLOW UP AND NEVER GIVE UP

No matter what business you have started, or what product or service you will ever sell, follow-up must be an ongoing activity. In the previous chapter we spoke a lot about the initial face-to-face contact with a potential customer. Whether the contact is face-to-face, or by phone or mail, the subsequent activity is always follow-up.

> **25** Send a thank-you note to your customers. Thank them for your time together and for the potential opportunity to work together.

In most instances, follow-up begins with a thank-you note. Since you are just starting your business, now would be a good time to stop by a gift shop or the stationery department of a store and purchase a box or two of simple but elegant thank-you notes. Avoid the types with birds and flowers. Keep it simple!

Before sending a proposal or any follow-up business material, send off a handwritten thank-you note. This will differentiate you from the competition, and make you appear sincere and trustworthy. Although it takes a few extra moments of time, think of it as an opportunity to again sell some good qualities about yourself and your business.

**26** Send a letter of proposal to the customer within two to three days of the initial presentation. After the customer has received it, call and use good open-ended questions, such as "What's the next step?" or "When can we begin working on this?"

After sending the initial thank-you note, the next step to effective follow-up is a well-written letter of proposal. Next, telephone the prospect a few days after he or she has received the proposal. Utilize good open-ended questions. Avoid close-ended questions.

But first, what makes for a good proposal? Besides including the particulars you have learned about your prospect at the initial presentation, use the following checklist to make sure your proposal has covered all the right bases.

## PROPOSAL CHECKLIST

- Explain the details of your product or service. What is the customer going to get for his or her money?
- Explain the outcomes. What are the benefits to the customer if he or she buys what you are selling?
- Detail the time frame involved. How long will it take from start to finish?
- Describe the total cost. How much will it cost for each component? Can some components be removed and the cost reduced?
- Set your terms. When are payments due? How long will you work? If you travel who will pay for the expenses?
- Explain the reporting relationship. Who will you report to? Who else will you interact with while delivering your product or service?
- Describe any additional phases, products and services. What else can you sell the customer that will fit in with his or her current needs?
- Detail your support system. How much support will the customer receive from you after the sale has been

completed? Is it phone support? Is it on-site support? Is it included in the initial cost or is it additional?

- Close for action. Ask in the last paragraph, "When can we get started?"
- Attach a list of references.

Following is a sample proposal I drafted for you. It will help you construct your own customer proposal. Read it carefully and determine how it can be edited and made to work for your needs.

## SAMPLE CUSTOMER PROPOSAL

February 25, 1998

Peter Friedrich
THE WILLIAM PENN INN
Route 200
Gwynedd, PA 19436

Dear Peter:
Thank you for the opportunity to meet you and your team last week. As I had mentioned in the card I sent after my stay, which I hope you have received by now, the room was wonderful and your kind hospitality was greatly appreciated.

With reference to our discussion concerning the strategic planning of your company's guest service mission, vision, culture and long-term development plans, the following reflects the proposed terms and conditions for our business relationship to facilitate this process.

**Phase One—Organization-wide Assessment**
The scope of the work will initially be Phase One, a survey assessment of the organization and a one-day senior team retreat to review the data and identify key issues.

**Components:**
- A one-on-one interview with yourself and each manager and supervisor
- A review of your existing customer feedback data
- Hand out a managerial skills and practices survey company-wide
- Implement an employee survey company-wide
- Provide all survey instruments
- Score all surveys
- Present to the executive team (possibly the expanded management team as well) the survey results report

**Outcome:**
- Identification of the current top issues facing the organization
- Identification of current culture, mission and values that have emerged
- Basis of creating a company-wide service culture, strategic development and change management plan. Begin to address key issues as they affect the customer and profitability.

**Time Frame:**
- All surveys distributed and returned    Two (2) weeks
- All surveys scored    Two (2) weeks
- Survey report prepared    One (1) week
- Executive team meeting    One (1) day

TOTAL:    Five (5) weeks and one (1) day

**Investment:**
- On site initial consultation (completed)    No charge
- Two-day management team one-on-one surveys    $ 1,400
- Survey instruments    1,400
- One week survey scoring    No charge
- One week preparing survey report    No charge
- One day on-site executive team meeting    700

TOTAL:    3,500

**Terms:**
To initiate an opportunity to work together, for phase one, an adjusted rate of $700.00 per day has been applied. To reserve on site-dates, compensa-

tion is due prior to the project's implementation. All checks are made payable to Gary Joseph Grappo, Personal I.D. # 421-32-3210.

In regards to travel expenses, reimbursement is requested for reasonable and customary expenses. An expense report with receipts will be submitted. This includes:

— Air travel round trip Ft. Lauderdale–Philadelphia
   Approximately $280.00 per round trip
— Ground transportation
   Approximately $30.00 per day car rental
— Meals
— Lodging

**Reporting Relationship:**
I will work as an independent contractor, reporting directly to you. I will have a close working relationship with other management team members as well as with supervisors and employees in the organization when necessary.

**Additional Phases Assure Long-Term Success**
As we discussed, there are other phases of implementation and follow-up after the assessment. They are necessary in order to assure long-term success of the key issues, guest service mission, vision, goals and actions identified at the executive team meeting. All the phases, when engaged, result in the implementation of a comprehensive service culture, change management and development plan for the organization company-wide. The follow-up phases can be discussed in depth during the phase one process. The following is a brief description of the additional phases:

**Phase II**
- Engage the management team in a one (1)-day retreat. Coordinate the following:
    — Finalize the key issues raised by the assessment report.
    — Facilitate solutions and actions around the key issues.
    — Facilitate a company vision and mission statement that reflects current strategic organizational goals.
    — Facilitate buy-in by senior managers and other key managers of key issues, goals, actions and direction.
    — Finalize solutions and actions necessary to address the top issues and their desired outcomes.

**Phase III**
- Write a first-draft annual strategic organizational development plan based on the survey results and management team retreat. Propose it to senior management as a *process* to create the desired guest service culture within the organization, resulting in increased guest and employee satisfaction, and measurable results to the bottom line.
- Co-write the final draft of the organizational development plan with the management team at a one-day retreat.
- Review the final draft and have the management team sign off on it at a half-day meeting.

**Phase IV**
- Coach, facilitate and nurture the complete organizational development plan and its process as agreed upon by the management team in its final draft. The process should include actions agreed upon in the phase one management team retreat as well as the following:
  — Training
  — Reinforcement
  — Reward and Recognition programs
  — Measurement
  — Appraising of the plan in each employee's review process
  — Disciplining of the plan for advancement
  — Employee recruitment that support the plan's objectives

**Support phase II, III and IV**
- On-site support for twelve (12) months for two (2) to four (4) days each month. Times may vary depending on your business levels. The Inn will be billed monthly at an agreed upon daily rate for these phases.
- Unlimited off-site phone support.
- Providing of Guest*Star, front-line customer service development training program that supports the organization's guest service development plan. Provides the following:
  — Guest*Star train-the-trainer
  — Unlimited copyright usage
  — Camera-ready participant's manual
  — Camera-ready leader's manual
  — Certification of trainers
- Train management to run the process by the end of all the phases.

**Extension**
This proposal expires at the end of phase one.
This proposal may also be extended and/or modified upon agreement in writing by both parties to accommodate the implementation of other phases described above.

Peter, once we complete phase one, as discussed, we'll have an opportunity to explain the benefits to the other team members in order to embark on the complete service culture development process encompassed in the other phases. When can we get started with phase one? Should you like to discuss scheduling or have further questions, I can be reached at 954/555-6265.

All the best,

Gary
Encls.

# REFERENCES

Mike Smith, Director of Human Resources
PENN STATE HOSPITALITY SERVICES
100 Park Street
State College, PA 16803
Phone: 814/555-7502

George Road, President and CEO
SCANCON INTERNATIONAL
200 Elm Road East
Princeton, NJ 08230
Phone: 609/555-8400

Paul Flower, President
ISLAND RESORTS
200 River Drive
Orlando, FL 33424
Phone: 800/555-3220

Peter Brown, President
GREEN HILLS HOTELS
High Ridge Street
Lake Ozark, MO 62101
Phone: 800/555-2700

Within three to five days of the arrival of your proposal, it is time for a follow-up phone call. The worst thing to do is to call with a close-ended question, such as "Did you receive my proposal?" Even though this mistake is made constantly by well-meaning business owners, why is this not a good approach? Because you are setting yourself up for a yes or no answer, and a conversation that will essentially go nowhere after the question is answered.

A better approach would be to call the prospect and ask a strong open-ended question, such as "What did you think of the proposal, and where do we go from here?" With this type of approach you have opened the phone call's conversation to endless possibilities where you can come out the winner.

In *Get the Job You Want in Thirty Days*, in regards to follow-up I state, "The main purpose of this type of follow-up is to take what I call 'a temperature check.' If the customer appears to be cold and indifferent, go on to other priorities. If the customer appears to be warm and enthusiastic, consider him or her a hot prospect and plan other forms of follow-up, such as another appointment to finalize the details, or dinner or lunch together. The follow-up possibilities for a warm prospect are endless."

Before calling, check your telephone skills. Always smile when speaking on the telephone; you've got to sound enthusiastic. One gentleman tells me his goal on the telephone is to have the energy level of Wally from the television show *Leave It to Beaver*. He is so right. Smiling while speaking on the telephone to a customer or prospect forces your voice to imply that your are an energetic and responsible person. Generally speaking, research has proven that people who smile have higher credibility.

**27** | **Love the word no. Learn to love rejection. The more no's, the closer you are to yes. It only takes one yes and you've got your first deal.**

Ten years ago, when I first launched my own business selling the training programs I wrote, TipsPlus, CareerEdge and Guest"Star my initial goal was to find a client, any client, who would say yes. That's all I wanted. I wasn't being unrealistic. I just wanted one person to say, "Yes, I want what you have."

In my mind, I surmised that it was a lot easier to concentrate on getting one yes than to focus on the huge task of selling enough business to pay bills and make a living. It also made sense to me. If I could get one yes, then that would indicate to me that there were others out there that would say yes as well.

So, after days of cold calling, and after a barrage of no's, I remained undeterred. I wanted one yes. And you know what? My formula worked. One day it happened. A restaurant on Key Biscayne hired me to train their food servers in my program TipsPlus. How exciting! Someone wanted to hire me. It's a great feeling to be wanted.

You will no doubt experience that feeling too if you reassess your attitude toward rejection. In the mind of small business owners there is no room for the word "failure". There are no failures. We believe each no, each rejection we get is simply a learning experience. Rejection helps us to refine our sales approach and our communication skills and ultimately bring us one step closer to success, a yes.

But how far do you go in following up? That is a constant question I hear from people who have to sell their business for a living. Sir Winston Churchill, in the heat of battle, in the middle of a war like none the world had ever seen before, answered that question. You may remember his now famous quote: "Never, never, never give up."

I had aggressively pursued one Fortune 500 company for more than a year before they became an exhibitor at my company's CareerEdge Job Fairs. The first time I called, the decision maker said, "We don't exhibit at job fairs." Giving me barely a chance to say good-bye, she hung up the phone. I remained resolute. Whether they knew it or not, I was determined that they were going to be my client someday. I made it a habit to call every month or so and just "touch base" with the key decision maker. Each time I squeaked a bit more information out of her and each time the phone calls remained short and abrupt. I remained resolute.

I kid you not, after one year or more of following up, she

broke. She finally admitted in one of my routine phone calls that all was not well in paradise. She admitted that the company's current recruitment methods were costly and not yielding enough results. She was ready to give CareerEdge Job Fairs a try. Long story short, her company eventually had a national contract with my company. When we saw each other, we would often laugh in hindsight about how long it took and how hard it was for me to finally get their business.

A lot of follow-up is based on a simple theory of just being in the right place at the right time. If you don't continue to follow up as in the case described above, you'll miss out on when the prospect is actually ready to buy. Your business will go to someone else if you don't get in the habit of loving no, loving rejection and remaining creative in your follow-up techniques.

## 28 Don't oversell. Learn when to shut up! Give a prospect the necessary room to process your proposal through his or her channels.

Whether at an initial customer presentation or in the follow-up stage with a customer, there is always the danger of overselling. If there is one lesson I have learned through the years it is this: learn when to shut up!

When selling your business, your enthusiasm needs to be tempered with organized and thoughtful communication. Be careful not to get on a tangent that leaves your prospect bored and suffused with so much information that he or she is no longer interested in your product. My problem and possibly yours at times has been to fall into the trap of talking too long because I am overly concerned about closing the deal, and becoming unfocused in my communication. We may want the business so badly that we keep talking to keep on selling. Although it sounds like the natural thing to do, don't. Keep your initial presentation and follow-up with a customer short and to the point.

Allow the customer the necessary time to process your proposal with other individuals who need to participate in the decision-making process. Instead of overselling the prospect in this situation, in hopes that he or she will go to the others to promote your deal, ask if the prospect would like you to come back and share your presentation with those who they feel are important in the decision-making process.

**29** Be flexible. Bend, shape, change and tailor your proposals to get the client's business. Get your foot in the door. What seems to be short-term loss could actually have long-term gain.

Be flexible. Once a client has received your proposal or ideas about how you expect to sell him or her your product or service, a certain amount of negotiating will inevitably take place. Unfortunately, I meet many small business owners who are not prepared to be flexible with their customers. Being inflexible is a guaranteed way to not make money and to get a bad reputation in the business community.

What I didn't tell you earlier about how I landed my first training product customer on Key Biscayne for TipsPlus was that I offered to do it for free! Now, is that flexible or what? The prospect was definitely interested in what I had to offer. The problem was that I had never done it before. I had no references. So you know what I did? I proposed that I offer to train their first group of twelve food servers for three hours in my program TipsPlus at no charge. In exchange I would get a certificate for dinner for two on an evening of my choice in their restaurant. It was a good deal. They got what they wanted, and I got what I wanted. That is what being flexible is all about. Don't be rigid. Make each of your customer negotiations a win-win situation. As a result of my being flexible, that customer became the reference I needed to begin selling TipsPlus for profit to other restaurants and hotels.

Often it is my habit in negotiating with prospective customers to bend over backward, to do whatever is necessary to get their business. In many cases, it is short-term loss for long-term gain. There have been many times in my business deals that I have initially taken much less for a product or service just to get my foot in the door. Once in the door, I have an opportunity to sell reliability, knowledge, attention to detail and all the other great things that people respect in a professional. As a result they keep giving me their business over and over.

> **30** Rely on this book's activity planner. There is no such thing as good luck. Rely totally on a good plan and good selling, and you will achieve your goal.

Immediately following is a thirty-day Activity Planner designed to go with this proven system. Doing the daily activities monitored in this plan is what's going to make you successful in starting and selling your own business. Taking action with the activities in this plan will make starting your own business now a more positive experience than any other attempts you may have tried in the past.

The readers of my thirty-day success systems account for hundreds and thousands of success stories. If you faithfully perform the activities and fill out this plan for the next thirty days, you will join them. Commit yourself to the effort described in the plan. Be relentless and determined to achieve your goal. With your determination and this plan, you will definitely come out a winner. Believe it. Visualize it. Never doubt it and you will make this book your success. Success. Yes, success!

Let's review what we have learned in this chapter:

25. Send a thank-you note.
26. Send a letter of proposal to the customer within two to three days of the initial presentation.
27. Remember the more no's you get, the closer you are to a yes.
28. Don't oversell. Learn when to shut up!
29. Be flexible. What seems to be short-term loss could actually have long-term gain.
30. Do not rely on luck. Rely on this book's Activity Planner.

# 7

# THE ACTIVITY PLANNER

Why are some people with high IQs considered unsuccessful, while others with seemingly lower IQs are extremely successful? According to Brian Tracy, the author of *The Psychology of Success*, IQ has nothing to do with success. According to Tracy, success is related to the number and quality of actions that an individual is willing to take in his or her life. He states, "No matter how smart you are, if you act stupidly, then you are stupid. Being successful has nothing to do with intelligence. If you act intelligently, then you are intelligent."

Because success is determined by taking action and not necessarily by intelligence alone, this book comes with an action-oriented Activity Planner. It is not enough to talk a good game or to just have good ideas. If that's all life is—discussions, ideas and theories—then getting to the next stage is never going to happen. Taking actions with calculated risks and making wise choices along the way will definitely get you anywhere you want to go.

The Activity Planner is what makes this system, *Start Your Own Business in Thirty Days,* effective. It is the only book of its kind that monitors key, critical small-business-ownership promotional activities on a daily basis. This book and the Activity Planner are practically the only tools you will ever need to start and run your own small business.

The Activity Planner also provides you with a concise synopsis of the thirty key concepts laid out in this book's success system. As you participate daily in the Activity Planner, you will notice that each day features a corresponding key concept that you learned earlier in the book. You won't have to sift through pages of information to remember the key points.

This Action Planner provides you with two attack options. The first is to work diligently promoting your business five days a week for thirty days. The second is to work nonstop, promoting your business seven days a week for thirty days. Deciding to work on your plan five days a week provides you at the end of thirty days with 200 new business contacts. However, for those of you with the time, to assure even greater success, I recommend pursuing the thirty-day-straight option. Here, you receive a total of 280 leads. Should you decide on this option, fill in the pages marked "Bonus

Days," to represent weekends. The difference between 200 and 280 could mean having or not having extra sales and cash flow to infuse your life and business with more money. Commit yourself to the extra work for thirty days if you can afford the time for the first few months of start-up. I don't recommend doing it much longer than that, for obvious health and family reasons. But, if you put in the extra effort, it will get your small business off and running in the right direction quickly and successfully.

This action plan also requires using your computer and the Internet where and whenever possible to help grow your business. To remain cutting edge and ahead of the competition, you need to commit to becoming completely techno-literate if your aren't already. For instance, this plan requires that you take the time to use e-mail to send follow-up messages to your prospects. By using your computer and accessing the Internet, you will be able to research your business and remain informed about its trends on a daily basis. You will even be able to use your computer and the Internet to generate leads and to network. There is a section in the Activity Planner to help you to do that.

The Internet activities are required bonus activities in order to diversify the promotion of your business. When possible and appropriate, make the additional investment to obtain your very own site on the Internet. Get the right advice. Be sure having a site on the Internet will help your business before making the investment. However important these Internet activities are, they do not replace the day-to-day conventional activities outlined in this plan.

Be aware that Day One represents a Monday. Begin your action plan on a Monday, when you are fresh and a new business week has begun. Also, it will keep the Bonus Days in line as weekends, should you decide to increase the quantity and quality of your success.

The Activity Planner is a step-by-step action plan that, when diligently followed, will get you customers, sales and cash flow in thirty days or less. Follow closely the steps listed here and fully complete the Activity Planner. The Activity Planner must be completed on a daily basis to assure that you are putting the proper amount of work and strategy into building your business. Remember, do not rely on good luck. Rely on a good plan—the Activity Planner.

## THE ACTIVITY PLANNER

## CHECK ATTITUDE

Today I practiced positive self-talk and visualization (check one)

- ❏ POSITIVE ALL DAY. I HAVE NO DOUBT I WILL SUCCEED.
- ❏ POSITIVE ONLY PART OF THE DAY. I'VE HAD MY DOUBTS.
- ❏ DOUBTFUL AND NEGATIVE MOST OF THE DAY.

## CHECK LEAD GENERATION
I discovered ten new hot prospects today (list below)

PERSON OR COMPANY NAME          PHONE NUMBER

1.

2.

3.

4.

5.

6.

7.

8.

9.

10.

## CHECK MARKETING LETTER

I sent marketing letters and a business card to all ten new hot prospects (list below)

| PERSON OR COMPANY NAME | ADDRESS | PHONE |
|---|---|---|
| 1. | | |
| 2. | | |
| 3. | | |
| 4. | | |
| 5. | | |
| 6. | | |
| 7. | | |
| 8. | | |
| 9. | | |
| 10. | | |

## CHECK CUSTOMER PRESENTATION

I practiced customer presentation role-plays with a friend
(list appointments)

| PERSON OR COMPANY NAME | PRESENTATION DATE & TIME |
|---|---|
| 1. | |
| 2. | |
| 3. | |

## CHECK FOLLOW-UP THANK-YOU
## NOTES AND PROPOSALS

Thank-you notes and proposals sent?   Yes_____   No_____

| PERSON OR COMPANY NAME | ADDRESS | PHONE |
|---|---|---|
| 1. | | |
| 2. | | |
| 3. | | |

## CHECK FOLLOW-UP PHONE CALLS

Follow-up phone calls made?    Yes_____    No_____

| PERSON OR COMPANY NAME | ADDRESS | PHONE |
| --- | --- | --- |
| 1. | | |
| 2. | | |
| 3. | | |

## CHECK FOLLOW-UP E-MAIL

Today, I utilized e-mail to follow-up with key customer prospects

| PERSON'S NAME | E-MAIL ADDRESS |
| --- | --- |
| 1. | |
| 2. | |
| 3. | |

## CHECK INTERNET WEB SITES

Today, I searched Internet sites related to my business and learned of three sites that can help give me information about my business or even provide me possible leads and networking.

| INTERNET SITE NAME | ADDRESS | OTHER INFORMATION |
|---|---|---|
| 1. | | |
| 2. | | |
| 3. | | |

## WEEK 1

### Day one

> **1** If you think you can or can't, in either case you're probably right.

### Day two

> **2** Practice positive self-talk: "I can! I will! I know I can do it!"

### Day three

> **3** Neutralize negative self-talk ("I'm worried. This business will never work") with positive winning statements.

## Day four

**4** Don't wait for others. Take personal responsibility for creating and implementing your own business.

## Day five

**5** Practice visualization. When you lie awake in the morning or evening, visualize working at and enjoying your own business.

## Bonus day six

6

Sell image! Dress like a winner. Shine your shoes. Have a conservative hairstyle. Design quality printed materials.

## Bonus day seven

7

Write a *simple* business plan. Include just enough information to prompt taking immediate action. Avoid becoming overwhelmed with too much planning and thus paralysis by analysis.

# WEEK 2

## Day eight

**8**

Choose a descriptive name for the business that creatively says exactly what the business does.

## Day nine

**9**

Define your vision. That is, answer the questions Why do we exist? What do we want to become in the future?

## Day ten

**10**

**Define your mission. That is, answer the questions How am I going to do it? How am I going to get there (to the vision)?**

## Day eleven

**11**

**Define your product or service.**

## Day twelve

**12**

**Know your costs. Answer the following: What are your costs? What are the client's costs? What is your profit?**

Bonus day thirteen

**13** Define your support staff needs and wages.

Bonus day fourteen

**14** Prepare a first-year budget.
Estimate numbers for the following:
- General operating expenses
- Equipment and capital expenditures
- Expected wages for support staff
- Expected sales
- Projected income from all sources

## WEEK THREE

### Day fifteen

**15** | **Learn about the competition.**

### Day sixteen

**16** | **Join the $50,000-a-year club! Secure ten new leads a day for your business; fifty a week.**

### Day seventeen

**17** | **Secure twenty contacts a week from cold calls. Simply drop in on twenty businesses or individuals who will benefit from your product or service. Get their names and addresses. Go back home and mail them a marketing letter. Better yet, try to see them while you are there.**

## Day eighteen

**18** Secure twenty contacts a week from calling businesses listed in directories such as the Yellow Pages, the Chamber of Commerce and association lists. Send them a marketing letter and business card after your call.

## Day nineteen

**19** Secure ten leads a week through networking. Attend business association meetings, community organizations and functions.

## Bonus day twenty

**20** Develop leads relentlessly—daily from 9 to 5 (if you are still at another job, on evenings and weekends)—until you achieve your sales goal. Do not waste business hours writing proposals, book-keeping or even washing your car.

## Bonus day twenty-one

**21** When selling your product or service, there are only two ways to learn about a customer's needs. Listen and ask good open-ended questions.

## WEEK THREE

### Day twenty-two

**22** Use role-plays to practice for a customer presentation the night before. Ask a friend to play the role of the customer.

### Day twenty-three

**23** Arrive at an appointment at least ten minutes early. If you arrive on time, you're late.

### Day twenty-four

**24** Do not discuss costs at the beginning of a presentation. Build value first.

Discuss general costs in the last few minutes of a presentation. Send detailed costs later in the form of a proposal or contract.

## Day twenty-five

**25** Send a thank-you note to your customers. Thank them for your time together and for the potential opportunity to work together.

## Day twenty-six

**26** Send a letter of proposal to the customer within two to three days of the initial presentation. After the customer has received it, call and use good open-ended questions, such as "What's the next step?" or "When can we begin working on this?"

## Bonus day twenty-seven

**27** Love the word no. Learn to love rejection. The more no's, the closer you are to yes. It only takes one yes and you've got your first deal.

## Bonus day twenty-eight

**28** Don't oversell. Learn when to shut up! Give a prospect the necessary room to process your proposal through his or her channels.

## WEEK FIVE

### Day twenty-nine

**29** **Be flexible. Bend, shape, change and tailor your proposals to get the client's business. Get your foot in the door. What seems to be short-term loss could actually have long-term gain.**

### Day thirty

**30** **Rely on this book's Activity Planner. There is no such thing as good luck. Rely totally on a good plan and good selling, and you will achieve your goal.**

# BIBLIOGRAPHY

Arden, Lynie. *The Work at Home Source Book*. Boulder, CO: Live Oak Publications, 1996.

Bautista, Veltisezar. *How to Build a Successful One-Person Business*. Farmington Hills, MI: Bookhaus Publishers, 1995.

Covey, Stephen R. *The 7 Habits of Highly Effective People*. New York: Fireside, 1990.

Elsea, Janet G. *The Four Minute Sell*. New York: Simon & Schuster, 1984.

Fisher, Lionel. *On Your Own*. Englewood Cliffs, NJ: Prentice Hall, 1995.

Fogg, Davis C. *Team-Based Strategic Planning.* New York, NY: AMACOM, 1994.

Fuller, Cheri. *Home Business Happiness.* Lancaster, PA: Starburst Publishers, 1996.

Gawain, Shakti. *Creative Visualization.* New York: Bantam Books, 1995.

Grappo, Gary Joseph. *The Top 10 Fears of Job Seekers.* New York: Berkley Books, 1996.

Grappo, Gary Joseph. *Get the Job You Want in Thirty Days.* New York: Berkley Books, 1997.

Grappo, Gary Joseph. *The Top 10 Career Strategies for the Year 2000 and Beyond.* New York: Berkley Books, 1997.

Helmstetter, Shad. *What to Say When You Talk to Yourself.* New York: Simon & Schuster, 1986.

Hill, Napoleon. *Think and Grow Rich.* New York: Fawcett Crest, 1988.

Hopkins, Tom. *How to Master the Art of Selling.* New York: Warner Books, 1982.

Liraz Publishing. *The Entrepreneur Test.* The Managing a Small Business CD-ROM: Liraz Publishing Co., 1996.

Liraz, Publishing. *The 30 Best Inspiring Anecdotes of All Times.* The Managing a Small Business CD-ROM: Liraz Publishing Co., 1996.

Lord, David. *National Business Employment Weekly Guide to Self-Employment*. New York: John Wiley and Sons, 1996.

Mehta, Stephanie N. "More Women Quit Lucrative Jobs to Start Their Own Businesses," *The Wall Street Journal*, November 11, 1996, page 1 (Eastern Edition, Orlando, FL).

Ramsey, Dan. *101 Best Weekend Businesses*. Franklin Lakes, NJ: Career Press, 1996.

Rooney, Andrew A. *The Most of Andy Rooney*. New York: Galahad Books, 1990.

Sinetar, Marsha. *Do What You Love, the Money Will Follow*. New York: Dell, 1989.

Schiffman, Stephen. *Cold Calling Techniques That Really Work*. Holbrook, MA: Adams Media Corporation, 1990.

Tracy, Brian. *The Science of Self-Confidence* (tape series). Solana Beach, CA: Brian Tracy, 1990.

"USA Today's Baby Boomer Panel...Woven With Threads of Diversity," *USA Today*, August 14, 1996, sec D.

"U.S. News & World Report's You Inc.," *U.S. News & World Report*, October 28, 1996, page 66.

Waitley, Dr. Denis. *The Psychology of Winning*. New York: Berkley Books, 1986.

# CORRESPOND WITH THE AUTHOR DIRECTLY ON THE INTERNET

Mr. Grappo appreciates hearing from readers of his books and participants in his seminars. Write when you have an experience to share. Success stories based on the use of his concepts are always welcome. Also, to order quantities of his books or to reach the author for a speaking engagement, write him on the Internet at the following address: ggrappo@mindspring.com. You can visit two of his business ventures, The American Hockey Association at http://www.americanhockey.net and ASTEC International Human Asset Technologies at http://www.careeredgeonline.com.